DR. ROGER J. WILLIAMS'
REVOLUTIONARY PROGRAM FOR
THE PREVENTION OF ALCOHOLISM
IS THE RESULT OF A LIFETIME
OF RESEARCH INTO ONE OF SOCIETY'S
MOST BAFFLING ILLNESSES.

In this book he offers heartening news to all who
have reason to fear the devastating results of
alcohol.

Dr. Williams has won world-wide recognition
through his pioneering work in the field of
vitamin research. In addition to concentrating
and naming folic acid, he was the first man to
identify and synthesize pantothenic acid, one of
the most important B vitamins. During his di-
rectorship of the Clayton Foundation Biochemical Institute from 1941 to 1963, more
vitamins and their variants were discovered than
in any other laboratory in the world. He is best
known to the lay public as the author of such
coast-to-coast bestsellers as *Nutrition in a Nutshell, Nutrition Against Disease* and *The Wonderful World Within You.*

The Prevention of Alcoholism Through Nutrition

by Roger J. Williams

Clayton Foundation Biochemical Institute
The University of Texas at Austin

Elkton, June '81

The opinions in this book belong exclusively to the author, and do not necessarily reflect the opinions of the publisher.

THE PREVENTION OF ALCOHOLISM THROUGH NUTRITION
A Bantam Book / July 1981

Table, "Range in Relative Organ Weights of Rabbits," from Wade H. Brown, Louise Pearce, and Chester M. Van Allen, Journal of Experimental Medicine; copyright 1926. By permission of The Rockefeller University Press.

Illustration, "Stomach, variations in form," from Atlas of Human Anatomy by Barry J. Anson; copyright 1951. By permission of W. B. Saunders Co.

Illustrations, "Taste Sensitivity" and "Urinary Constituents" from Biochemical Studies IV, University of Texas, May 1959.

ISBN 0–553–14502–9

Published simultaneously in the United States and Canada

Bantam Books are published by Bantam Books, Inc. Its trademark, consisting of the words "Bantam Books" and the portrayal of a bantam, is Registered in U.S. Patent and Trademark Office and in other countries. Marca Registrada. Bantam Books, Inc., 666 Fifth Avenue, New York, New York 10103.

PRINTED IN THE UNITED STATES OF AMERICA

0 9 8 7 6 5 4 3

ACKNOWLEDGEMENTS

Due to my eyesight disability in recent years there have been a number of people who contributed magnificently toward making the production of this book possible.

I am gratefully indebted to my wife, other family members, my colleagues and associates at The University of Texas, Anita Brewer of Austin, Texas, and my agent, James C.G. Conniff of Upper Montclair, New Jersey, all of whom have given invaluable help.

Professor William Shive has acted as a frequent consultant. He not only discovered the glutamine effect, but his help has been invaluable because he is an expert and knows as much about the intricate chemical workings of the human body as anyone I know of.

My friend and ally, Mr. R. Brinkley Smithers, President of the Christopher D. Smithers Foundation in New York, has written a Foreword for this book and has helped greatly in other ways. He has helped me get valuable suggestions about the content of the book from Dr. Ernest Noble of the University of California, Irvine, and Attorney George Pidot, whose help I acknowledge with thanks.

My immediate colleagues and associates at The University of Texas, Drs. Donald R. Davis and Man-Li S. Yew and Mrs. Marguerite M. Biesele, have contributed mightily. Mrs. Biesele has ably and graciously taken on the major task of getting the manuscript in shape. Mrs. Esther Eakin has also devotedly helped me on this and other writing projects

Finally, I wish to thank in advance the many physicians who will cooperate to supervise the prevention procedure in individual cases.

Roger J. Williams
November 7, 1980

Contents

Foreword

This book succeeds admirably in presenting in layman's terms information on nutrition that *if followed* should prevent alcoholism and many alcohol-related problems from developing, even in those who choose to drink alcoholic beverages. It will help in practically every case because, as Dr. Williams has made clear, it is impossible to maintain an excellent nutritional status while drinking heavily, and experts agree that heavy drinking is usually an essential prelude for the development of alcoholism.

Alcoholism is a many-sided malady, which, in one way or another, adversely affects almost every human activity in the Western world.

Dr. Williams, a pioneer in the field of nutrition, has shown that every human being is, in terms of his biochemistry, innately highly distinctive. In other words, no two individuals are identical in bodily structure, and neither are their chemical processes always carried out in the same ways. This being the case, different persons need different combinations and amounts of food elements—vitamins and other nutrients.

You will find in reading this book that many guidelines are suggested, and if followed, your general health and that of your loved ones will be better served and susceptibility to alcoholism will be eradicated or greatly reduced.

Probably the main point to make here is that the less "junky," overprocessed food and soft drinks that are consumed by young people, the less chance there will be for alcoholism or heavy drinking in later life. This is due to the fact that the food that youngsters eat contains too much sugar. If they switch to alcoholic beverages in later life, the alcohol works like the sugar did in their earlier food—except more so. As Ogden Nash, the humorist, said, "Candy is dandy, but liquor is quicker."

As president of the Christopher D. Smithers Foundation, I have had the pleasure of working with Dr. Roger Williams and the Clayton Foundation since we put on a joint symposium on the "Biochemical and Nutritional Aspects of Alcoholism" in October, 1964. Since that time, our Foundation has become more and more concerned with the *prevention* of alcoholism, as we have found that treatment alone is not sufficient. More alcoholics are being made by society and problem drinking among our young people is increasing at an alarming rate, with the result that, despite a wider application of treatment, the total number of active alcoholics has not decreased. It is our opinion that *prevention* is and must be *the* answer, and one of the main tools toward achieving that end is seeing that people are properly nourished. This should start when the child is still in its mother's womb and continue through life.

Of course, hereditary factors undoubtedly play a strong part in developing alcoholism, and persons with close alcoholic relatives may be much more susceptible than others. This high risk population would be better off never drinking and if they do, they should not take their first drink until they are at least twenty-one years of age.

The reader, I believe, will find this book of immeasurable value, and as the saying goes, "It will make you feel your oats."

R. Brinkley Smithers
President
The Christopher D. Smithers
Foundation

To the Reader:

This book was written for all those who want to know effective ways to prevent alcoholism in themselves and for those, including professional consultants, who wish to prevent it in loved ones and others. Almost everyone is touched by this disease directly or indirectly at some stage of his or her life. **Everybody** should have some grasp of how alcoholism may be prevented.

In the interests of the people they serve, physicians, psychiatrists, psychologists, ministers, priests, rabbis, counselors, and educators need to know the basic principles underlying the prevention of alcoholism.

Great inroads with respect to this disease cannot be made until the general public is well informed. We desperately need to develop the psychology of expecting each member of society to take serious responsibility for his or her own welfare and for being well informed on matters related to individual health.

The Prevention of Alcoholism Through Nutrition presents the insights of the author based upon his lifetime study of nutrition and its vital connection to the health of the individual. It does not purport to give medical advice. The author advises that the whole prevention procedure be under the supervision of physicians, many of whom, in the 1980's, have become sympathetic and cooperative with the objectives set forth in this book.

Preface

This book deals with the devastating problem of alcoholism in three unprecedented ways.

1. With no wasted words, it tells in straightforward, practical terms what one can do to attain alcoholism prevention most effectively. What you will find in these pages will make complete sense. Moreover, you will be able to follow the recommendations. There is nothing outlandish here, nothing beyond the reach of any man or woman, young or old.

2. In ways that self-styled experts rarely discuss—because these experts simply don't have the information this book contains—the pages that follow will show you how and why *prevention* is the only sane approach to the problem of alcoholism. Preventing the problem from ever arising could save this nation billions of dollars annually, and untold heartache.

3. The book gives the layman background information that will make it clear how the disease we call alcoholism starts, and why the "experts" of past decades have done such an unsatisfactory job of helping people cope with it. You will see evidence that alcoholism is a baffling metabolic disorder that slowly, soon ferociously, and often fatally, attacks individuals who are vulnerable to it but who have never learned the simple facts about how they can protect themselves against it.

Most people, including the experts, have no grasp of the metabolic details involved in individual cases of alcoholism. Aggravating that fact is the further unfortunate fact that there are all too few investigators who have the know-how to evaluate the problem in critical terms that could help potential victims.

Such an investigator would have to have a working knowledge of (1) the biochemical intricacies of metabolism, (2) the exacting processes of cellular nutrition and general pathology, and (3) the inescapable vagaries of individual metabolism.

Most medical scientists tend to neglect or ignore these time-consuming subjects. I know, because at every opportunity that came my way during the past thirty years and more, I have invited them to pay more attention to these vital insights into the causes of alcoholism and the means available to prevent it from ever developing.

I again extend that invitation. In the pages that follow, I present new material clarifying the deeper meaning of metabolism, how alcoholism promotes general cell sickness (cytopathy), a new suggested strategy for the conduct of medical research, and a critical review and evaluation of the alcoholism research carried on in various parts of the world. With this material in mind my readers will want to join their voices with my own in *demanding* a more constructive approach to the prevention of alcoholism at the individual, national, and international levels.

My credentials on which the writing of this book is based include the fact that I have discovered some of the important vitamins which are essential to alcohol metabolism, have paid a great deal of attention to the complexities of metabolism in human bodies, and have written the only published book dealing with biochemical individuality, the vital basis upon which the existence of the disease, alcoholism, rests. Other writers on the subject of alcoholism have their own valid credentials but none of their credentials are in any sense similar to mine.

As a result of my particular background I have an excellent picture of the scenario of what happens metabolically when an individual becomes an alcoholic. My strategy is to prevent the events which are preliminary to alcoholism from taking place. The full details of how alcoholism develops in an individual case are necessarily distinctive in each instance, and science has not progressed to the point where anyone knows fully what these details are. The nature of the general picture, however, is such that I feel certain that we now know scientifically how to prevent alcoholism and what remains is to get people informed and motivated to avoid the pitfalls.

Part I

Steps to Prevent Alcoholism Most Effectively

Preamble
What the Important
Message Is

Ten million people in our country are in serious trouble with alcohol. They drifted, slipped, or slid into this trouble—sometimes gradually, always sadly. They represent ten million individual stories of torment, lost marriages, broken lives, loneliness, unrealized dreams, and mislaid promises. Each alcoholic has a tragic story all his or her own.

The contents of this book are crucial to all these stories. If most of these individuals at an early age had known and followed what we present here, their bouts with alcoholism and its attendant griefs might never have happened. In the light of modern knowledge—which as yet is not adequately applied—we can avoid alcoholism by the exercise of well-informed common sense. Without exercising superhuman strength or unusual power, any person can avoid becoming entangled in the morass of alcoholism.

I will now proceed in chapters 1 through 7 to discuss the seven effective measures that individuals can take to prevent alcoholism. Each of these measures will be helpful by itself; taken all together, they will enhance the probability of success.

1

Treat Yourself As
the Unique Individual
You Really Are

There are two prime factors that enter into alcoholism. One is *alcohol*, the other is *you*. Prevention involves taking stock of yourself and getting acquainted with the fact that you are a unique, special person—with a distinctive makeup, with distinctive likes, dislikes, and needs. Because of your uniqueness, you must do many things *for yourself*. You have many self-responsibilities because there is no one else to shoulder them.

The late John Knowles, famous physician and president of the Rockefeller Foundation, once wisely proposed that it is manifestly unfair for any member of society to eat and drink irresponsibly, smoke irresponsibly, and drive with abandon and then expect the medical profession and society to come to the rescue and take care of the dire consequences.

If you are really serious in your desire to prevent alcoholism you will carefully study yourself and seek to understand the nature of the malady you are trying to prevent.

If you do not appreciate your own individuality and instead measure yourself by others, as many do, you are in for trouble. You cannot properly take any of the measures I discuss in the following six chapters unless at the outset you recognize your own uniqueness.

While people often resemble each other in many

aspects of their makeup, they are never really alike. When you were born you already had a distinctive nervous system and brain, a unique set of endocrine glands, a distinctive stomach and digestive system, a unique heart and circulatory system. You were also distinctive in your body chemistry and in many other ways. For more information on this subject see the bibliography in Appendix III.

Some people have biochemical makeups that make it extremely unlikely that they will ever become alcoholics. Others have characteristics that make it very easy for them to drift in this direction. There are all kinds of gradations in between these extremes. These are facts one needs to know if he or she is to be fully successful in preventing the disease of alcoholism.

People differ enormously in the way they respond to alcohol. Some can drink and drink and never get drunk, seeming to possess "hollow legs." This is a dangerous situation because such individuals have no natural protection against the poisoning effects of large amounts of alcohol. Others can take one drink and to them the world appears dimmer and often seems to whirl and rock. These individuals are better protected from large amounts of alcohol because they are not likely to drink as much—a little of it seems to go a long way.

A medical report (Jetter) describes remarkable results from an experiment in which one thousand persons cited for drunken driving were tested in two ways: (1) how well they could walk a chalk line, etc., and (2) how much alcohol was in their blood. These tests provided information about how much alcohol in the blood, *on the average*, brought on intoxication. The study, however, went deeper into the problem and recorded the results of both tests for each person individually. The results were amazing.

Some individuals were *intoxicated* when the blood alcohol level was very low—0.05 percent. At the other extreme, using the same criteria, some were *sober* when the alcohol content in the blood was very high— 0.4 percent. Even with eight times as much alcohol in their blood as their inebriated brothers, these superficially hardy specimens still seemed unaffected. Some of them had almost enough alcohol in their blood to have killed the least resistant persons. However, such apparently resistant individuals are very likely to suffer from chronic alcoholism because while they withstand high levels of alcohol concentration for a short time, prolonged use may do severe damage.

Proneness to alcoholism is a highly individual matter. In alcoholism deep-seated toxic effects occur and radically change one's personality. Although almost anyone can become an alcoholic if he or she uses enough alcohol for a long enough time, the range of vulnerability to this disease is enormous.

In order to keep on good terms with alcohol one must get acquainted with one's self in relation to the effects of alcohol. If you have alcoholic parents, or if alcoholism runs in your family, you are a high-risk individual—in other words, statistically you are more liable than most to become an alcoholic. Perhaps it would be wisest if you abstained from alcohol altogether. This is *your* responsibility. Certainly, as we shall see later, high-risk individuals should consistently cultivate moderation. If you like alcoholic drinks very much (often people do not), this increases your risk and you must guard yourself accordingly.

If one drink always calls for a follow-up of another drink, this is a danger sign and you will do well to pay attention to it. If you are a young person (perhaps a teenager), this alone makes you more vulnerable. At this stage of life, when one is still growing and developing, everyone is more alcoholism-prone than he or she will be when he or she has matured. This is why children and youngsters should abstain from alcohol entirely, and young people should at least cultivate extreme moderation.

Because each of us is an individual, the effects of alcohol consumption vary from person to person in almost infinite diversity.

Alcohol consumption can give a person a feeling of euphoria and well-being. It is a "social lubricant"; it can sometimes help one forget troubles and be optimistic. One of the world's great men, Winston

Churchill, said, "I have taken more good from alcohol than alcohol has taken from me." This, of course, was one man's opinion, based on his individual experience. For persons with constitutions very different from Churchill's to follow his example with respect to liquor might be disastrous. Benjamin Franklin expressed a contrary view when he said, "Drinking does not drown care, it waters it and makes it grow." Each individual person may have quite a different experience with the same alcohol consumption. For some, drinking alcohol makes laughter easier and people more affable and friendly. Jokes may seem funnier than usual. Other drinkers grow sleepy, some become weepy, and some get fighting mad at the slightest provocation. Some become talkative, some sing, and some are sullen.

Alcohol at a high enough level is poisonous. The fact that it may be *toxic* is inherent in the word *intoxication,* used to describe alcohol's effect when the level in the blood affects a person's performance.

The effects of alcoholic intoxication are numerous. A famous scientist, a Nobel laureate, told me jokingly in Copenhagen that he could never become an alcoholic because when he consumes even a little alcohol he immediately becomes nauseated and vomits. Vomiting is one sign of intoxication, but it is far from a consistent signal. Other signals associated with alcoholism—again far from consistent—may include slurred speech, loss of sense of balance, double vision, headaches, and extreme sensitivity to loud noises. Double vision is a symptom of severe intoxication, as also are indirectly "the shakes," delirium, and stupor. In these symptomatic variations, alcohol has seriously deranged the brain function.

Intoxicating effects of alcohol can cause a great variety of physiological and psychological troubles. Liver disease (cirrhosis) is a common companion of alcoholism and receives considerable attention. The severity of the liver disease, however, is not always parallel to the severity of alcoholism. Unfortunately, the investigator studying liver disease accompanying alcoholism may concentrate on the liver rather than on the alcoholism. While many of the problems cousin to alcoholism may merit study, working the side streets will not adequately explore the alcohol problem itself.

The most serious toxic effect of alcohol, and one that experts have not clearly recognized, is the derangement of the appetite mechanism located in the hypothalamus of the brain. It is serious because loss of appetite leads a person into a vicious cycle from which escape is difficult or impossible.

Nowhere is individuality more important than in the study of the appetite mechanism as related to alcoholism. Some individuals can consume alcohol regularly and heavily for years and still maintain a relatively normal appetite mechanism. They may have a stronger desire to drink than others, but they still crave and eat reasonably adequate food. Food consumption serves to protect them from the severest derangement. Other drinkers quickly lose their appetite for food. They drink heavily, they lose their appetite for food, and then they want to drink more and more, and eat less and less. In the most severe cases, the susceptible individual loses all appetite for food. The sight and smell of food become repulsive, leaving nothing but a craving for alcohol. Such a severe condition leads to death within a short time. The environment of the brain cells becomes so deteriorated that normal brain functions cease. If you find that alcohol consumption decreases your appetite, this is a danger signal you should watch.

Appetite derangements, common among alcoholics, are rare but not unknown in other diseases. In diabetes, for example, the individual diabetic may abnormally crave sugar, something that physiologically the diabetic cannot handle properly. This abnormal craving for sugar by a "sugar-sick" individual is somewhat parallel to the strong craving for alcohol by an "alcohol-sick" person.

Pharmacologists know beyond doubt that innate differences exist in susceptibility not only to alcohol but also to poisoning by different drugs and chemicals. One can demonstrate this with as many drugs as one wishes to test—caffeine, nicotine, chloroform, quinine, novocaine, aspirin, alcohol, etc. You as an individual have a distinctive pattern of susceptibilities towards dozens of drugs. This is why, when entering a hospital as a patient, one of the first questions asked is, "Are you 'allergic' to any specific drug or medicine?" This, too, is why competent physicians have to know what medication you are taking before prescribing something else.

The moral is: Do not compare your alcohol capacity with what Sadie Jenkins or Sam Hawkins drinks. Every person has a distinctive pattern of physiological and psychological reactions to alcohol. There is no connection between how some other individual reacts and how you react. To overlook this fact is a grave blunder and may cause you to build your life plan on a false foundation.

In the preamble to this book I wrote, "In the light of modern knowledge—which as yet is not adequately applied—we can avoid alcoholism by the exercise of well-informed common sense." One of the vital ways to exercise common sense and to ensure avoiding trouble with alcohol is to appreciate the facts of individuality and incorporate them into action. The mere memorizing of certain phrases or maxims will do no good. *One must live like an individual and reject the brainwashing arising from those who believe that people are carbon copies of each other.*

People are individuals with respect to their following or leading others. Some are prone to be like sheep and follow any suggestion that comes along (if others drink, they drink too); some are comfortable living their lives as though they had a duty to be circumspect at all times and to do only what others regard as appropriate; some are much more inclined to "kick over the traces" and adopt a don't-care attitude towards what others think and do; some want to be "leaders of the pack."

The consumption of alcohol is an activity in which each individual must learn to be himself or herself and play his or her own game.

The degree of trouble experienced with alcohol varies tremendously from individual to individual. Some people are addicts and yet are "light drinkers" when compared with those who drink the most. Some, without previous experience, like alcohol immensely. Robert E. Lee said of alcohol, "I like it; I always did, and that is the reason I never use it." Some learn to like the effects of alcohol by practice. Some drink heavily for a time and then automatically go on the water wagon for a few weeks. Some alcoholics are drunk most of the time; some are almost never drunk but still go on binges they seem to be unable to avoid. Just as there is no such thing as *the* alcoholic, there are no prescribed stepping-stones to alcoholism. Thus, each person must learn for himself which paths are dangerous.

Thomas Fuller has said, "Alcohol is a turncoat; first a friend, then an enemy." This doesn't have to be. The purpose of this book is to show how it is possible, by exercising well-informed care, *for anyone who is not already an alcoholic* to keep on friendly terms with alcohol. You will succeed in doing this only if you carefully recognize your own uniqueness and take on your own unique responsibility.

One of the important things you need to know about if you are to protect yourself from alcoholism is your own unique *internal environment*. The meaning of the expression "internal environment" will be made clear in the following paragraphs.

Each of us starts life as a tiny, fertilized egg about the diameter of the shank of a pin. When the much tinier sperm cell fertilized the egg cell from which you came, this settled your heredity with finality. From this point on, environment became the big question mark. Give this tiny fertilized egg cell the right environment and it will develop into a healthy, whole human being and everything will be lovely.

A very important part of this environment is the supply of oxygen, water, and forty or more nutrients (see p. 21), *each one of which* is essential to life. The egg cell from which you came was, for genetic reasons, a distinctive one. It had a pattern of needs that was different, in that the quantities of the different nutrients needed were unique. The fertilized egg that became you had peculiarities and vulnerabilities different from those of other individual eggs. This is where individuality starts. No fertilized egg receives perfect conditions throughout life. The only practical way this initial fertilized egg can get an adequate environment is by nurturing it in the womb of the mother-to-be.

From conception to the cradle to the grave we must have at least a passable nutritional environment if life is to continue. In the womb a mechanism develops whereby the blood of the healthy mother provides the growing fetus with an *internal environment* that supplies the growing cells and tissues within the fetus with every nutrient it needs. The mother, in order to provide this internal environment, must consume the right nutrients in about the right amounts.

When you were born the word "environment" took on new meaning because of the outside world and everything and everybody in it. Despite the fact that this outside world environment is highly important to the newborn baby, its internal environment still must remain adequate at all times if life is to continue.

The ordinary nursing infant gets the forty or more needed nutrients through its mother's milk (if she is healthy), but when the infant begins to eat more or less indiscriminately, the internal environment may become far from ideal. This is particularly true if sugar, white flour products, and white rice are a substantial part of the diet.

If you—as a special, growing youngster—received poor nourishment, you became, for this reason, more susceptible to alcoholism and now have a special need to be careful.

While our internal environment must be at least passable every day and every minute of our entire lives, during youth and development this environment is particularly crucial. If one's internal environment were really good from the period of babyhood through adolescence, we would form habits that would largely take care of us the rest of our lives. Unfortunately, however, this is usually not the case, and many of our ailments and troubles in later life develop because of lapses in our internal environment during this critical period.

We all need oxygen to breathe and water to drink— these are fundamental. However, oxygen and water constitute but the tip of the iceberg of our internal environmental needs. Our need for oxygen is continuous; we need it every minute. If we lack oxygen for even a few minutes, we die or suffer brain damage. We cannot store oxygen supplies in our bodies or put them on reserve. Water is just as necessary as oxygen for life, but we can last for hours or days without an environmental supply because our bodies do contain water reserves. Many other items in our environmental iceberg are like water in that we can store them in varying degrees and do not have to replenish the supply every minute as we must do with oxygen. However, we do *need* the other items in the environmental iceberg every minute and every second of our lives. Unless we store them we are goners.

Though immeasurably more complex, human bodies are something like automobiles. An automobile, to run, needs environmental oxygen second by second and gets it through the carburetor; if the oxygen supply is cut off, the engine stops instantaneously. An automobile, however, when its gasoline tank is full, can travel two hundred miles or more without a need for *fuel* from the environment. It carries part of its environment with it and gets its oxygen from the air.

In addition to oxygen, water, and fuel to burn, our bodies must have the minerals, amino acids, and vitamins we have listed on page 21. We often overlook these chemical needs because they are not obvious like the need for oxygen and water. We have some storage capacity for these chemicals, thus we may not need to replenish some of them very often. However, *they must be available at all times*.

The need for these chemicals is basic. Human beings can and have lived without the trappings of civilization that we regard as fundamental—houses, clothing, means of transportation, education, books—yet no human being historically or prehistorically has ever lived without a supply of these approximately forty "iceberg" chemicals, which are essential to human internal environments.

We derive oxygen from our environment through our noses or mouths. We drink water. We eat the tissues of plants and animals to obtain the essential chemicals. But merely eating something or other does not ensure that we receive the chemicals we need. It is a sad mistake to believe that we get them all automatically in the right amounts whenever we eat any old thing the food merchants might offer. The food may taste deceptively good and be next to worthless.

Environments are never perfect. You have never lived, I venture, in a region where the climate is always ideal—where the temperature, day and night, summer and winter, is exactly right, as well as the humidity, wind, rainfall, and sunshine. I venture to suggest, also, that you have never lived in a neighborhood where all the neighbors and their cats and dogs behaved perfectly, or where the social influences and educational opportunities were perfect.

Nature does not provide us with perfect foods, so—like our external environments—our internal environments are often far from perfect. You have never in your whole life consistently consumed exactly the right amounts of the essential chemicals.

After each item in the list of essential nutrients (p. 21) is indicated, in parentheses, an estimated average daily human need for that nutrient. These amounts, all thirty-nine of them, do not apply to you. In your present state of health, which is probably not optimal, you have a unique internal environment that is a part of you. Some of your needs may be well in excess of those indicated, and your inner environment probably is not keeping pace with all of your needs. Unfortunately, medical science has not developed to the point where you can know exactly what all your needs are and how far short your environment is in matching your needs. If you knew yourself perfectly, you would know about your needs and your internal environment and the solution to your nutritional problems would be easy. Even the Roman, Lucretius, over two thousand years ago realized that individual needs are not all the same. He said, "What is one man's meat may be another's poison."

Why do we need these hidden chemicals, and what do we do with them when they enter our bodies?

We use them to keep the intricate machinery of our bodies running efficiently, so this machinery—like our cars—can work for us. Every cell and tissue in every organ and structure of our bodies contains this marvelous life machinery. The forty chemicals serve as "building blocks" for this incredibly complex machinery.

If any link in the essential chain is missing, the machinery stops as surely as it would if oxygen were lacking. We have trillions of living cells in our bodies. Some cells work with more efficiency than others, and some need different nutrients than others. The internal environments with which we surround the various tissues, through the food we eat, are not necessarily equally good, equally bad, or even equally mediocre for all the different kinds of cells. Also, because our circulatory systems are distinctive in anatomy, some persons are built so they feed their brains—and other cells of their bodies—much better than others do. Some individuals have larger and more effectively branched blood vessels to feed their brains, or their hearts may be better pumps.

If it were possible to take a "metabolic x-ray" of you, showing your internal nourishment, we might find an overall, barely passing grade of sixty percent efficiency; or we might find a ninety percent metabolic efficiency depending largely on your individual vulnerabilities and your choices of food.

To merely stay alive, the cells and tissues of our bodies do not require anything like perfect nutrition. Cells and tissues and organs in the bodies of individual persons often limp along, "getting by" as best they can.

Giving every cell of the body an excellent environment containing every one of the nutrient chemicals in the right amounts is a tremendous logistic operation. We can never attain such perfection. We certainly do not even approach it when we eat carelessly and do not provide our blood with a good assortment of health-giving nutrients.

Why is it that we get all these necessary chemicals (but not necessarily in the right amounts) whenever we eat the tissues of plants and animals? The answer is simple: *Life machinery* is present in every living thing, and life machinery, wherever it exists always contains the same basic materials. The essential chemicals thus are ubiquitous in the life machinery of all plants and animals. There is a marvelous unity in nature.

Our ultimate goal is the prevention of alcoholism. We cannot possibly attain this goal unless we guard, cherish, and build up our *internal environment*. This is something over which we have control. Each person has, in his or her present state of health, a unique environment, which, however, is subject to change and improvement. All of the six measures we will discuss in the following chapters have as their object the improvement of internal environments. If you wish to prevent alcoholism, you will adopt these measures, bearing in mind the fact that after conception (when your heredity is established) environment is all we have to work with.

If you fully realize your position as a unique individual with unique responsibilities, this may give you a psychological lift and a determination to meet the problem of preventing alcoholism head-on. If you have digested the contents of this chapter, you have reason to be of good cheer. Testing of alcoholics for the quality of their internal environments *invariably* shows them to be deficient in several respects. If you keep your internal environment from seriously deteriorating, you will never become an alcoholic.

2

Eat High Quality Foods

Eat like a responsible individual. Do not follow someone else's lead; instead, try to take care of your own
bodily requirements.

A transformation in your life can take place if you
build up and improve your inner environment. Your
body is a marvelous machine made up of a multitude
of coordinated cells and tissues, which work together
to give you health and keep you free from disease.
But when one link in this chain of cells and tissues
begins to ail or malfunction, your whole body suffers.

These cells and tissues make life and health possible, and all they ask of you is *a good environment*.
The heredity of these cells and tissues usually is
good enough so that everything will run smoothly if
you give them a good place to live.

Building an inner environment to avoid future trouble is not magic, and anyone who cares enough to be
well informed and reasonably kind to his or her body
can do it. Unfortunately, many persons are careless
about the way they treat their body machinery. Ray
Lyman Wilbur, a renowned physician who was president of Stanford University for many years, said:

> "Most people have but little idea how to care for
> their bodies or how to use their brains and be well
> and happy. Millions of them keep themselves
> under the partial influence of caffeine, alcohol,
> nicotine, aspirin, and other drugs a good deal of

16

the time. From childhood they never play fair with the finest machine on earth. The doctors themselves are not always good examples, and many of them care for their automobiles better than they do for themselves."

One outstanding way to play fair with your "finest machine on earth" is to concentrate on eating high quality foods.

As we have noted, nature never provides us with perfect foods. Some, however, are of higher quality than others. Eggs, for example, are of very high quality because they contain within one capsule *everything* necessary to build a complete baby chick. One of the reasons eggs are not a perfect food for human beings is that they lack vitamin C. Some nutritionists object to eggs as a human food because they contain substantial amounts of cholesterol. This objection is invalid, however, because cholesterol is an essential substance, particularly in brain tissue, and it is only when cholesterol blocks blood vessels that it is damaging. This problem is by no means a simple one. For rats, which do not require vitamin C in their diet, eggs are about the most perfect food that exists. Milk is, practically speaking, a perfect food for young animals, but it does not contain enough iron and other trace minerals for adults. If eggs and milk agree with you and you like them, they are highly recommended foods. Some people cannot tolerate them, however, and this changes the picture entirely. We are individuals in our eating as well as in many other respects. About ten percent of Caucasian adults and about forty percent of Negro and Oriental adults cannot tolerate more than minimal amounts of milk because they lack in their digestive tracts the enzyme lactase that makes possible the utilization of milk sugar, lactose.

Fortunately, there are many other high quality foods to choose from. These include the tissues of plants and animals and the products derived from them without emasculation: meats, fish, shellfish, cheeses, vegetables (peas, beans, carrots, potatoes, tomatoes, corn, cabbage, lettuce, spinach, mushrooms), fruits (oranges, apples, bananas, melons, berries), and whole cereal products derived from rice, wheat, corn, oats, buckwheat, etc. Every one of these foods—and those similar to them—contains a good assortment of the hidden chemicals (p. 21) required in internal human environments.

It is quite unnecessary to prescribe specific menus for your breakfast, lunch, and dinner because people have different inclinations and tastes, and there are many ways that we can prepare high quality foods without destroying their value. No one should have to consume food that he or she finds unattractive or distasteful.

In selecting the high quality foods you eat, take into consideration the following:

- Diversify. Do not concentrate on single foods to the exclusion of others. In this way you are likely to get a better assortment of the hidden chemicals you need.

- Eat the high quality foods you like. If you are reasonably healthy, you probably have some "body wisdom" that helps you select what you as an individual need.

- Eat foods that your body accepts without complaint. You should avoid foods that disturb your sleep, cause constipation, diarrhea, nausea, headaches, or skin reactions.

- Think of the cost. Some foods are far more expensive than others of similar quality. Low income people need to exercise extra care to get the most for their money.

The building up of your internal environment will take some time—more than just a few days. Eating high quality food will bring results in time, but the other measures I will discuss later will speed up the process. Eventually all of the measures I suggest should be taken concurrently.

3

Avoid Low Quality Foods

When you consume *only* high quality foods, you automatically exclude all low quality foods—those that yield poor assortments of the necessary maintenance chemicals (p. 21). Unfortunately, many poor or mediocre foods are on the market, and some of them taste very good indeed. Those who are anxious to avoid problems with alcohol should avoid eating substantial amounts of low quality or mediocre foods, no matter how attractive they are.

Excess sugar is one of the chief enemies of good inner nutritional environments. We promote its excessive use by doing such things as adding sugar to baby food formulas, offering sugary breakfast foods to children, floating our pancakes in syrup, glazing doughnuts with a thick crust of sugar, serving candied sweet potatoes, using extra sugar in a host of foods, widely displaying and selling candies, candy bars, and soft drinks, and customarily offering sugary desserts at the conclusion of a meal. Those who wish to build strong inner environments should keep the consumption of sugar to a minimum. It is easy and satisfying to avoid excessive sugar once a person accustoms himself to lower levels of sweetness. Sugar furnishes calories, sweetness, and energy but *no* maintenance chemicals (p. 21). It crowds out of the diet high quality foods, which are relatively rich in these maintenance chemicals. Although it is better for a potential alcoholic to drink a soft drink than an alcoholic beverage, the sugar-containing drinks do nothing to build up inner environments.

White rice, white flour, refined fats, and alcohol itself are also enemies of those who want to improve the quality of their inner environments, and the problem is made more acute because we often use these products in relatively large quantities. From the standpoint of furnishing the hidden chemicals needed in life-machinery, white flour and white rice are roughly one third to one half as valuable as the original grains from which they came.

Foreign chemicals in our foods can also impair internal environments. Many experiments have shown that impaired internal environments cause rats to increase their alcohol consumption. Investigators found, in a 1972 study, that rats consumed three times as much alcohol when caffeine (coffee) was added to their diet. Since rats are probably more susceptible to caffeine poisoning than humans, this observation should not be regarded as proof that caffeine is conductive to alcohol consumption in human beings. It does suggest, however, that foreign chemicals may act in this way.

Related to the importance of avoiding poor quality foods is the problem of obesity. This is a weight-conscious age and eating too much concerns many people. This danger decreases, however, if the *quality* of one's food is excellent. The vast majority of those who have to fight to keep their weight down do three things wrong: (1) they fail to concentrate on high quality foods, (2) they fail to avoid the poorer and totally inadequate foods, and (3) they fail to exercise sufficiently.

To eat and satisfy energy needs is a strong biological urge. Most of us satisfy these needs almost automatically. Many troubles arise, however, when we eat foods that merely furnish energy and do not include the vital hidden chemicals that make cellular life and health possible. One of the troubles that arises this way is alcoholism.

In summary, concentrating on good foods and keeping the use of poor foods to a minimum will, by themselves, help prevent the development of alcoholism.

The outstandingly poor foods are sugary drinks, candies, cakes, sugar-enriched desserts, and starchy snacks such as soda crackers.

ESSENTIAL "ICEBERG" NUTRIENT CHEMICAL NEEDS

Amino Acids

Isoleucine	(0.8 gm)	Phenylalanine	(1.1 gm)
Leucine	(1.1 gm)	Threonine	(0.5 gm)
Lysine	(1.5 gm)	Tryptophan	(0.25 gm)
Methionine	(1.1 gm)	Valine	(1.0 gm)

Major Minerals

Calcium	(0.8 gm)	Magnesium	(0.35 gm)
Chloride	(7.0 gm)	Sodium	(5.0 gm)
Potassium	(4.0 gm)	Phosphate	(2.0 gm)

Trace Elements

Cobalt	(0.1 mg)	Iodine	(01. mg)
Chromium	(2.0 mg)	Manganese	(5.0 mg)
Copper	(2.0 mg)	Molybdenum	(0.5 mg)
Fluorine	(0.5 mg)	Selenium	(0.5 mg)
Iron	(15.0 mg)	Zinc	(15.0 mg)

Vitamins

Vitamin A (alcohol form)	(1.5 mg)	Folic acid	(0.4 mg)
		Vitamin K	(2.0 mg)
Biotin	(0.3 mg)	Niacinamide	(20.0 mg)
Vitamin B_6	(2.0 mg)	Pantothenic acid	(10.0 mg)
Vitamin B_{12}	(0.006 mg)	Riboflavin	(1.7 mg)
Vitamin C	(60.0 mg)	Thiamin	(1.5)
Vitamin D	(0.01 mg)	(vitamin B_1)	
Vitamin E (tocopherol)	(30.0 mg)		

Other

Choline	(1.0 gm)	Linoleic acid	(5.0 gm)

These nutrient chemicals are absolutely essential for life and health and must be furnished in our daily food. Next to each chemical listed is an estimated, approximate daily requirement for the chemical in question. (These needs may vary substantially from individual to individual.)

4

Exercise to Promote
Internal Nutrition

If a person spends most of his or her time sitting or lying down, rarely getting the exercise he or she biologically requires, this person will have poor circulation and hence be poorly nourished even though he or she eats plenty of good food and little poor food. If the nutrients from good foods do not reach our cells and tissues, we will be poorly nourished no matter what we eat. Without exercise, the whole system tends to stagnate.

Every person has his own individual pattern of blood vessels, thus internal nutrition, coming from eaten food, will be distinctively different from person to person. If a person's blood circulation is poor, this may shortchange some cells and tissues continuously. Poor blood circulation may often cause brain impairment.

Thus, in addition to good food, a person needs adequate exercise. We should remember we are biological creatures, adapted to being physically active. In primitive times everyone was continuously active procuring daily food and shelter. We have not changed biologically since those primitive times. We still need exercise to keep our circulation in tune. Circulation—which we can improve by exercise—is the only way necessary nutrients can reach all parts of our bodies, including our brains.

Just what "adequate exercise" means is difficult to

define because what would be adequate for some might be inadequate for others. If a person walks or jogs several miles a day, his or her exercise is certainly above average. People in general would probably be better off if they were doing something physically almost every hour of the day. The kinds of exercise that people may take are numerous. Some people prefer to exercise vigorously for a short time only, while others take much more moderate exercise for longer periods of time until they are physically tired but not exhausted. The type of exercise and the amount must be left largely up to each individual. I believe everyone will be able to recognize and take advantage of the improvement of his or her health resulting from additional exercise.

A report has come to me of one individual who solved his small problem with drinking merely by taking up jogging. It is probable that anyone who has even a slight problem with alcohol will find the problem lessened by walking or jogging for extra exercise each day. This alone will help strengthen one's internal environment.

It is notable that many persons who live sedentary lives are vulnerable to alcoholism. Writers, actors and actresses, lawyers, politicians, and others who often are inactive physically are vulnerable, particularly when they also are affluent and can afford to loaf—and drink. Many of these individuals would lose their vulnerability if they routinely engaged in physical exercise, thus strengthening their internal environments.

In organized retirement areas, the very nature of the communities often helps breed alcoholism. When affluence is the norm, with it often comes bridge with drinking, golf with drinking, boredom with drinking, but very little jogging, hewing of stone, drawing of water, and chopping of wood. Retirement should *always* be accompanied by regular physical exercise.

The good effects of adequate exercise will usually be felt almost immediately. One must move into an exercise program gradually and not allow enthusiasm for exercise to carry him or her to extremes. Moderate but fully appropriate exercise, taken regularly, will do wonders for many people, and they will not have to wait for months to see the effects.

Exercise is an extremely important help in preventing alcoholism. Most alcoholics do not consistently take vigorous daily exercise.

5

Cultivate Moderation—
and Inner Peace

Many of you who read this book drink alcoholic beverages, at least occasionally. You probably wish to continue to drink. This is entirely possible, but I would urge you to cultivate moderation *while you can.* After a person becomes an alcoholic, he will not, and literally *cannot,* listen to such words as "caution" or "moderation."

The surest way to avoid the threat of alcoholism is to abstain from the use of alcohol. This is a price most are unwilling to pay. It is quite possible, however, to be happy without alcohol. If you are afraid that a small problem may become serious, you may wish to abstain now, while you still can. One of my close friends, an executive in a responsible position, had such a strong liking for alcohol that he was afraid of it and did not drink at all. He gave cocktail parties, kept liquor in his locker at the club and offered it to his friends, but he never drank with them. He recognized that he was an individual and, as an individual, thought it best that he not drink.

An alternative to abstinence is moderation. I believe this course is open to the vast majority of adults, provided they use caution and develop understanding of how important it is to maintain a healthy internal environment, particularly for the appetite-regulating cells in the brain.

There is no rule of thumb for how much is safe for

any one individual to drink and it is impossible to define moderation with one formula. An amount of alcohol quite safe for one individual may be unsafe for another. There is one principle, however, which may safely be followed by every person: If your taking one drink demands another and another, you had better watch out. You are in danger of reaching the point where the decision to take another drink is out of your hands—when the tyranny of addiction will take over. The sooner you recognize the need to watch the internal environment, the better. Childhood is none too soon.

Psychological difficulties often accompany an increasing desire to drink. Those who have inner peace of mind are less vulnerable. Accordingly, it is most desirable for a person having trouble with alcohol to seek to cultivate this peace of mind by any means at his or her disposal. Because people have such different personalities and attitudes, specific advice for each person is difficult to formulate. Reliance on religious faith, talking with friends, consulting with psychologists all may be valuable expedients for different persons. Clearing his or her own conscience and avoiding trying to be someone other than his or her better self are important starts. Building wholesome attitudes and a healthy personality goes hand in hand with building a superior inner environment.

The disease of alcoholism does not usually strike suddenly and without warning. Practice feeds the disease and the training for alcoholism usually covers a period of several years. During this time the candidate for alcoholism feels sure he or she can stop whenever he or she wishes, but *gradually*, as heavy drinking continues, this ability to stop is lost. The time to cut down on drinking is in the early stages when the self is in control.

Two courses are open to every consumer of alcoholic beverages, whether male or female, young, middle-aged, or elderly. One course is to drink on and on without inhibition or restrictions and without regard for the quality of his or her internal environment. This course may lead into a *vicious cycle*. The more drinking, the more the internal environment deteriorates. This promotes further drinking and further deterioration of the internal environment. And so, on and on, and the ultimate result, if the process is unchecked, is death from alcoholism.

Happily, nature helps us tremendously if we take the other course—the course of applying caution and being watchful of our internal environments by demanding the right nutrients for our systems and ensuring that a healthy circulation delivers them to our cells. The more one follows this course, the easier, more attractive, and health-giving it becomes. Health begets health. Eating good food promotes better food selection. Getting good exercise makes exercise more natural and easy. Craving for liquor does not dominate one's life. One thus sets in motion a marvelous beneficial cycle.

The environment of our brain cells is crucial. From the standpoint of movement, the brain seems a quiescent organ. Chemically, however, it is extremely active. Although the brain weight is only about two percent of that of the whole body, the chemical burning that takes place in the brain may be twenty-five percent of the total chemical burning in the body. The brain is metabolically a hot spot. This copious burning is not just happenstance, but is absolutely essential to life, health, and the operation of numerous regulatory mechanisms that promote moderation and balance.

On the average, an adult loses about two thousand brain cells each hour—indicating that the environmental conditions in the brains of most persons are far from perfect. At this rate perhaps one-eighth of one's total brain cells would be lost during forty years of adulthood, and unlike liver cells, blood cells, and many other body cells, nerve cells are not automatically replaced when they become worn out. Certainly, if their environment were perfect, these cells would not die off. The two thousand brain cell deaths an hour is an average figure. In some individuals, the brain cells die off faster than in others. In alcoholics the brain cells must die off much, much faster. In a South Carolina medical school, students could not use the brains of alcoholics after death for dissection. The brains had lost most of their structure and were like mush.

Individuality is most important in cultivating moderation. The reasons persons unwittingly prepare themselves for future trouble with alcohol are individual reasons. Some like (or love) alcohol and what it does for them at the start and forever after. Some start out drinking to be "one of the crowd," whether they like alcoholic drinks or not. Some who wind up being alcoholics never like the taste of alcoholic drinks, but they take them as a medicine to help them forget their troubles, overcome their inhibitions, or banish their guilty feelings.

It is a fact of life that some individuals, because of their inborn characteristics, are far more prone to become alcoholics than others. Most persons can become alcoholics if they are induced to drink heavily and consistently for a long time, whatever the reason. For some, it is vastly easier to fall into the trap than it is for others. Some can drink regularly and heavily for many years without becoming typical addicts, and then succumb to the disease of alcoholism in their declining years. Virtually no one is safe if he or she fails to provide a sound environment for the cells of the brain.

Most unfortunately, young people and teenagers become addicted relatively quickly. For young and growing individuals, the inner environment is crucially important. They need the hidden chemicals at higher levels than adults because growth as well as maintenance is a part of their lives. I have heard it said that if a person becomes an alcoholic before the age of twenty-eight there is no hope of recovery. The importance of preventing alcoholism in young people cannot be overstated.

Psychology and emotions are important factors in cultivating moderation in drinking. These areas are complex, as each person—with or without problems—is an individual whose personality is not like anyone else's. In spite of the large amount of talk and discussion about the psychological aspects of alcoholism, the disease marches on, trapping more and more people. Discussions that leave out biochemical and psychological individuality are ineffective in preventing the disease.

Alcoholics Anonymous has done wonders for a great many afflicted alcoholics. Whether it is its philosophy or its method of operation or a combination of the two, the organization accomplishes something very positive for those it helps. They encourage alcoholics to sober up and to leave alcohol alone. The victims begin eating. Whatever they eat, even if it is of inferior quality, is bound to begin to build up the inner environment. Thus, the quality of the environment goes uphill and continues to do so as long as they leave alcohol alone.

The limitation of the Alcoholics Anonymous program is that it starts with sick people (alcoholics) rather than well ones. It does not purport to achieve prevention but only recovery. It does nothing to prevent the early deterioration of the internal environment. This deterioration finally leads to a climax of alcoholism—the loss of self-control. Alcoholics Anonymous does some marvelous salvage work; however, disaster precedes the salvage. Waiting until one becomes helplessly alcoholic before taking action is like waiting until one's house is fully ablaze before calling the fire department.

The strategy that I recommend is to use effective measures long before serious difficulties arise and thereby prevent potential alcoholics from ever becoming actual victims. The fires of alcoholism may have small beginnings, which the potential victim can snuff out early while he still has a high degree of self-control.

Prevention of alcoholism in teenagers is an acute problem, which only education of both children and their parents, and nonnagging, nonpunitive, intelligent attitudes on the part of concerned adults can solve. The social climate in which youngsters grow up often makes it appear "manly" or "womanly" to drink freely. We need, instead, to develop an atmosphere in which it is far more mature to stand on one's own legs and get along without the crutch of alcohol. The host or hostess who encourages guests to drink "one more" and "one more" and "one more" is exhibiting a kind of hospitality that leads to hospitalization. Alcoholism breeds in such a climate.

Maturity is an important part of life—a goal young people strive for. No one can blame youngsters for wanting to grow up and appear mature. If we can educate young people (and their parents) to know they (1) are individuals, (2) have internal environments that require watching, and (3) are, in a large measure, responsible for their own lives, they too can avoid serious problems with alcohol. They, above all others, need to abstain, or exercise extreme moderation, in addition to eating the right foods and keeping fit through exercise.

—more", and "one more", and "one more" is sought, a
a kind of hospitalization. Man's second chance has

6

Use Nutritional
Supplements

In addition to eating the right foods, exercising adequately, and cultivating moderation, using nutritional supplements (see Appendix I) may be extremely helpful for some individuals for whom alcoholism poses a serious threat. Why not protect one's internal environment by consuming in the form of tablets, capsules, or "elixirs" some of the hidden chemicals that may be lacking in his or her body? It is desirable that a person specifically seeking to avoid alcoholism do so under the supervision of a licensed physician. Many physicians have now become sympathetic to the nutritional approach.

To protect one's internal environment perfectly is difficult. I have, however, developed a formula which I recommend for avoiding alcoholism (see p. 116, Appendix I). For most individuals this supplement covers twenty-six kinds of possible deficiencies. I have no financial interest whatever in this or any other nutritional supplement. I have made this formula available free to manufacturers and the public.

Taking this "Currently Suggested Formulation for Nutritional Insurance" regularly will materially help some individuals with alcohol problems almost immediately, that is, within a few weeks—especially if they follow the suggestions we have already given in the first five chapters. This is a formula that, preferably under medical supervision, any adult or adolescent can take, or smaller children, who can take the same in doses one-third as large. It helps to build and maintain the internal environment of those who take it, and in many cases a person can advantageously continue its use indefinitely.

There are some individuals who may have higher requirements than this supplement supplies. For those who are in immediate danger of becoming alcoholics, I recommend the "Currently Suggested *Fortified* Formulation for Nutritional Insurance," which contains much higher amounts of some of the vitamins and double the amount of some of the minerals and other nutrients (see Appendix I, p. 117). If one tolerates this fortified supplement well, he or she can take it indefinitely, but in many cases it may be desirable to continue it at a lower level.

In taking supplements, it is most important that one takes them regularly. It is better to take them with meals, but the time of day is less important than the regularity. Some individuals can take supplements regularly three times a day, but others, if they attempt to do this, end up taking the supplements only occasionally. For them it is better to take the whole supplement at one time each day.

Consuming plenty of good quality protein is the best way to guard against deficiencies of amino acids. The vast majority of us can improve our internal environments without the use of amino acid supplements, which are expensive and present problems involving proper balance.

In spite of the widely held view that alcoholism is fundamentally a psychological problem, I can fully justify my emphasis on the biochemical and physiological aspects. Even if an inability to cope adequately with stress and tension (psychological problems) causes alcoholism, a biochemical improvement of the internal environment can greatly lessen stress and tension and banish pathological worry. Improving one's internal environment is the best method of attacking alcoholism in any case, whether the disease is caused by physiological and biochemical imbalances or by psychological stresses. Some would emphasize that "if a person is sound psychologically, he or she will not become an alcoholic." My position is that no person can be sound psychologically unless the day-by-day internal environment surrounding the brain cells is of appropriate high quality.

If any of my readers can find benefit from a psychological or religious attack on problems related to alcohol, well and good. In those cases, direct biochemical improvement of the internal environment of the brain cells will bring *additional* relief.

If you succeed in preventing alcoholism in yourself, the story will not make the newspapers. But, your whole outlook on life will change, your psychology will change. You will go about your business without any hoopla and without worrying about how bad off you might have been if you had resisted good advice.

Nutritional investigators have performed "miracles" many times in recent history:

- By giving sufferers from pellagra good food and ensuring a good supply of niacinamide, doctors have eliminated the deadly symptoms. They have taken victims—run-down, emaciated, suffering from diarrhea and hallucinations—and transformed them into healthy, happy individuals, free from disease and mental aberrations (insanity), within a few weeks or even in a few days.

- By giving good food—including plenty of vitamin D, calcium, and phosphate—to rickety, weak, and wobbly children with abnormal bone growth, they have changed them into strong and healthy children with normal bone growth in a few months.

- They have taken paralyzed and weak victims of beriberi, suffering with loss of appetite, and transformed them, using good food including vitamin B_1, into healthy specimens.

- They have "doctored" victims of scurvy with good food and vitamin C and have brought them back to health.

- They have treated victims of pernicious anemia—who were threatened by death—with good food and vitamin B_{12} and cancelled out the disease and its threat.
- They have given good protein food to potbellied, dull children suffering from kwashiorkor and changed them into healthy youngsters with all the normal potentialities.

These facts and hundreds of others, plus insights into the interplay of heredity and environment, convince me that any individual on the road to becoming an alcoholic but not yet there can leave this road and take the road toward health simply by ensuring the cells of his or her body a good supply of all the essential, needed nutrients. This will be a miracle no less than those cited above. The potential victim will be rid of his or her psychological troubles and of his or her abnormal thirst for alcohol.

Years ago, a university student, hearing of my interest in and work with alcoholism, asked if I could help him. He was not a long-standing alcoholic, but he had lost a job because of drinking and he complained to me that he couldn't seem to leave alcohol alone. The only thing I could offer him was an experimental nutritional supplement, which I gave him.

Reports came back to me that the supplement was working. On one occasion, my colleague observed the student in a beer parlor nursing one bottle of beer for hours instead of drinking to excess. The student called me eighteen months later. Speaking of the nutritional supplement, he said, "It has been like a miracle in my life. When I take it regularly, I have no trouble at all staying away from liquor." It is evident to me that the particular supplement that I gave him hit the spot in his individual case. For another individual we might have to try a somewhat different supplement.

One of those who took nutritional supplements in accordance with my recommendations did so under the supervision of a physician in a California hospital. It happened this way: This middle-aged, successful professional man suffered from high blood pressure and could get no relief. A medical clinic advised him to take barbiturates "to calm his nerves." He did so. Later, on top of taking huge doses of barbiturates, he began drinking heavily. Finally he ended up in a California hospital, far from home, physically down and out.

His drying-out period was gruesome. However, the physician in charge contacted me and followed my suggestions with remarkable success. After drying out and taking generous nutritional supplements for a few weeks, the patient was able to leave the hospital and return to work in his law office. His blood pressure had dropped to 130/90. He had lost his craving for alcohol and his dependence on barbiturates. I chanced to visit him nearly a year later, and he was getting along fine, with none of his former troubles. Here again the nutritional supplement, which he had continued to take, hit the spot.

While we cannot count on the same supplement to bring such dramatic results in all cases, this one case shows what nutritional supplements can sometimes do. If a nutritional supplement can help an extreme case like this, the chances of nutritional supplements helping those with minor troubles are excellent.

Unfortunately, some persons are prone to disregard minor problems until they grow into major ones. Among my numerous contacts was a prominent, All-American collegiate athlete. He had an excellent physique and handled himself beautifully in most respects. However, he had a slight problem with alcohol and "watered it" with plenty of whiskey. He not only maintained a friendship with alcohol, he let it become his one and only bosom friend, displacing all his other interests. He did not care about sex, his family or church, business—where he had excellent prospects—or politics. All he cared about was alcohol and his drinking associations. At the time that I knew his family best, he did not want help. Drinking was his life. But his life didn't last very long. He died at an early age from the effects of alcoholism.

This is a scenario I hope my readers will avoid—

moderate drinking, followed by heavy drinking, followed by complete absorption with alcohol, followed by early death. This can happen to vulnerable individuals regardless of other circumstances. More than ninety percent of all alcoholics appear to be well-to-do, respectable persons, often with important jobs. You don't have to end up in the gutter to be an alcoholic.

I will next discuss one further tool available to improve one's internal nutritional environment. This too may assist you in avoiding the perils of alcoholism.

7

Use Glutamine as a Supplementary Food

Several years ago my colleague, Professor William Shive, discovered, in a unique way, a connection between a lack of glutamine and problems with alcohol.

While studying the poisoning effect of alcohol on bacterial cells, he noted that there was *something* present in extracts of liver, cabbage, and other natural products that protected bacterial cells against alcohol's poisoning effect. When he added this *something* to culture media, the bacterial cells multiplied readily in the presence of otherwise intolerable concentrations of alcohol.

After many months of careful detective work Professor Shive found that the *something* in the various natural sources was glutamine, an amino acid. Alcohol normally interferes with certain bacterial metabolic activities. But when Professor Shive added tiny amounts of glutamine to the culture medium, the glutamine cancelled the effect of the alcohol, and the bacteria grew ten times as well in the alcohol solution as they did in the absence of glutamine. Following this striking observation, we experimented to find out if glutamine had any comparable protective action when fed to experimental animals.

Earlier we had observed that rats on relatively poor diets consistently consumed, by choice, relatively large quantities of alcohol. When we gave such rats glutamine, however, their voluntary alcohol consumption decreased about forty percent. This was an effect specific to glutamine. Other amino acids were completely ineffective. It was evident that glutamine partially protected the rats by causing them to drink less.

After finding that glutamine protects bacterial cells against alcohol, and also in a different way protects rats against alcohol, the next step was to see if glutamine also protects human beings. A physician of our acquaintance conducted a striking experiment. He decided to treat a confirmed woman alcoholic with glutamine without her knowledge. Glutamine is tasteless, so the doctor was able to get glutamine into her drinking water without her knowing anything about it.

The experiment was a tremendous success. After a few weeks, this confirmed alcoholic who had been completely worthless to society and to herself told her family, "I'm going to stop drinking." She then stopped. After several weeks of sobriety she took a job and continued to live the life of a sober person, without the desire to drink.

Glutamine has helped hundreds of alcoholics to my own personal knowledge. Unfortunately, however, it does not work like magic in a dependable fashion. Persons are unique in the details of their metabolism, so we cannot expect them to react in an identical manner to a particular agent. Your physician should be consulted before you turn to this approach.

One of the many thousands to whom we have sent information about alcoholism (without cost) wrote to me twenty-five years after her first inquiry and sent me her case history, which follows.

One Case History

I started drinking socially and very moderately at about age twenty-three. Before that time I would occasionally have a glass of beer with my family (parents) but much preferred chocolate fudge or ice cream with rich toppings, I'd say, inordinately. Fortunately, I stayed slim in spite of these indulgences, probably because of vigorous physical activities: tennis, golf, walking, biking, and dancing.

Before I married I traveled as a special representative in the cosmetic business, and it was part of my job to entertain often at cocktail parties and lunch, etc. This I took in stride. After getting married my husband's business involved much entertaining, and he often expressed complimentary observations on "how well I handled my drinks."

I believe that I remember the invisible line that AA defines as the crossover into compulsive drinking. It was on New Year's Day, 1956. We were expecting many guests for dinner, they arrived early; my nerves were jangling, I had a dreadful hangover, and looked to a drink for the solution. When the first drink didn't help, it seemed a different attitude was initiated in hurrying to have a second and stronger drink. This became a pattern.

To the surprise of my husband and family, I joined AA in November of '57. I believe, as I look back, that I was more of a potential alcoholic (I dislike that nebulous word) and hence didn't take it as a matter of life or death. Also, I was ensconced in a happy home with a devoted husband and two sons, and obviously my drinking had not reached a stage that was of concern to my husband, and he enjoyed our drinking together. He never over drank, he just enjoyed it. But inside myself I felt guilt, remorse, extreme nervousness, anxieties, and tried to treat these with alcohol to be comfortable enough to function, which of course did not work, and my response to self treatment was unpredictable.

Because of my dilemma and intuitive feeling that my problem was primarily biochemical, I read every book on nutrition that I could find. References in several of the books to Dr. Roger Williams led me to the book *Biochemical Individuality*. It was at this point that I called Dr. Williams. By return mail, I received the pamphlet "For Those Who Have an Alcohol Problem."

THIS MADE THE DIFFERENCE. Glutamine removed the compulsion to drink, and the prescribed nutritional recommendations restored good health. And time marched smoothly on.

By now our sons were leaving for college, and my husband and I were ready to resume our courtship with plans to go to Europe to celebrate our twenty-fifth wedding anniversary. They had both been away just two weeks, when my husband died suddenly of an aortic aneurysm while we were driving to have lunch. Of course this devastated me. I drank. I was in such shock, the drinking seemed to just keep me on level, without deleterious effects or overt signs.

I was not taking glutamine at the time because I had neglected to restock and had run out of it.

With urgency, I ordered glutamine and resumed all the things that I had learned about nutrition, etc., sort of by rote. Thus, with heavy reliance on spiritual concepts, again the desire to drink was dispelled, and gradually a sense of acceptance and courage followed.

Beyond any question, I feel the published recommendations of Dr. Roger Williams saw me through what seemed to be an impossible crisis. It confirmed a philosophy that I had spoken of but had not previously experienced at depth, that in this world we need to maintain training and conditioning like a boxer before a big fight. Sadly, my guard was down at the time.

I have since continued the glutamine, the vitamin and mineral supplements and try for optimal nutritional nourishment, with a minimum of carbohydrates.

I am in good health and find it more interesting and rewarding NOT to drink, than to drink. For this I am grateful.

Dorothy G. Beebe
425 Chilian Way
Palm Beach, Florida 33480

Because the professional counselors concerned with alcoholism are often completely unprepared to grasp the fundamentals of human metabolism and nutrition and because those in medical science have placed little importance on nutritional concepts for many decades, we have imperfect knowledge about the possibilities that glutamine offers.

In the past, traditional psychiatrists, whom alcoholics have often consulted, were by training unprepared to consider nutritional factors. They often regarded proposals in this area as puzzling and confusing—as mysterious as if in a foreign language. I personally know of two prominent psychiatrists, national leaders in the field of alcoholism, who shrugged off the use of glutamine on the basis of some very limited tests they made, both erroneously using *glutamic acid* instead of glutamine. (Glutamic acid is a totally different substance, which Professor Shive found ineffective as a substitute for glutamine.) This is past history now. It happened twenty or more years ago but could not happen now.

A new breed of psychiatrists, members of the Academy of Orthomolecular Psychiatry, founded in London in 1971, are very receptive to the consideration of nutritional factors in alcoholism and mental disease. These forward-looking psychiatrists constitute a great hope for the future.

Glutamine is a natural substance, which is present in every healthy human body. It is in no sense a drug. Our bodies produce it and hence it is not one of the essential nutrients that we must always get from the outside world. It is an amino acid and a "building stone" present in proteins.

Although our bodies produce glutamine, they may not always produce it in optimal amounts in all bodies; thus, certain individuals may suffer from a glutamine deficiency. In these cases glutamine supplements may be a valuable nutritional agent. Glutamine's relation to brain metabolism is particularly interesting because it is the only amino acid that readily passes the blood-brain barrier, a barrier that tends to stop many constituents of the blood, including most amino acids, from passing readily into the brain. Glutamine is an exception. Uniquely, it can serve as a source of energy for brain metabolism.

We do not know what proportion of the persons with alcohol problems glutamine will benefit. Every concerned person should give it a try after consulting his or her physician. Its high cost for many years (about $170 per ounce) prevented its common use. A daily dose, two grams (usually in divided doses), previously cost about $12. A daily dose now costs about twenty cents, so cost is no longer a reason to neglect its use. (Half a level teaspoonful weighs *approximately* two grams.)

Many unexplored possibilities for glutamine may exist. According to studies by Professor Shive in collaboration with clinicians, glutamine may have several additional beneficial effects. It may raise the I.Q. of small children. It may help to induce restful sleep. It speeds the healing of gastric ulcers.

Glutamine is a nutrient, not a drug, and from what we know is not dangerous in larger amounts than the common daily dose of two grams. Divided doses, one-half gram taken an hour after meals and before retiring, seem to bring the best results. It dissolves easily in water or fruit juice; it is available as a powder or in tablets or capsules (see Appendix I for sources). One should not heat it in solution or cook it with food because heating destroys it.

Glutamine is worth trying when alcohol consumption threatens to become a problem. For many, it curbs their unhealthy drive to drink. It should be used as long as it appears to be effective. No prescription is necessary to obtain glutamine, since it is a nutrient, not a drug.

8

Summation of Preventive Measures

I have now outlined seven measures for preventing trouble with alcohol: Treat yourself as the individual you really are (chapter 1), eat high quality foods (chapter 2), avoid low quality foods (chapter 3), exercise to promote internal nutrition (chapter 4), cultivate moderation—and inner peace (chapter 5), use nutritional supplements (chapter 6), and use glutamine as a supplementary food (chapter 7).

I advise everyone who cares about his or her health and about the immediate possibility of an alcoholic problem to adopt *every one* of the seven measures. However, each measure, by itself, may be helpful. Human nature being what it is, I know that some individuals will naturally play favorites and take some of the recommendations more seriously than others. In any case, I wish you luck. For those who are on the road to alcoholism, I urge that you do everything you can to head off this terrible disease. Remember, these different measures reinforce one another and are cumulative in their beneficial effects. It may take all seven measures to help you. (See p. 00 regarding supervision by physician.)

I am fully confident that *every person* who makes a serious effort to follow the suggestions outlined will receive benefits. Most of these suggestions are good for everyone, even those for whom alcohol consumption carries no threat.

In a later section of this book I will present further supporting evidence for the value of these preventive measures. This supporting evidence has its basis in the fundamental biochemistry involved in the alcoholism problem.

Points to ponder:

1. In my extensive experience in the field of nutrition and in attempting to combat alcoholism, I have never known anyone to become an alcoholic who has followed our recommendations even approximately. Statistically speaking, very few people indeed intelligently watch their nutrition (which includes moderation and exercise). Of those who do, I believe not one has ever become an alcoholic.

2. Every person who has become an alcoholic has developed an internal environment nutritionally deficient in several respects. This is corroborated by laboratory tests on many alcoholics.

Part II

Prevention the Only
Sensible Course

9

Why and When to Employ Prevention?

In the previous chapters I presented seven specific measures for preventing the onset of alcoholism. In your specific case, the earlier you apply these measures, the more certain will be success. Prevention is always simpler and easier than correcting or curing. Remember the adage: "A stitch in time saves nine."

Fire *prevention* is a sensible course, and technology exists to prevent fires—using fire-resistant materials in construction and furnishing, installing sprinkler systems in public buildings and smoke alarms in private homes; keeping trash and inflammable materials at a minimum, enforcing household rules forbidding smoking in bed also helps. We can easily put out a small fire; we can likewise banish a small tendency to drink too much if we start early. One can easily snuff out the fire from a single match. If we have a flaming skillet or a blazing curtain, these are manageable if we act in the right way immediately. But if we procrastinate and delay, the fire may get out of control and we may lose the whole house.

We need to prevent alcoholism in its early beginnings. If we wait "to see what happens" week after week and month after month, it may be too late and we may destroy our lives.

Not only is prevention of alcoholism a sensible course, but the prevention of disease in general is the best way to be and remain healthy. Doctors perform their best service, and people benefit most, when they prevent smallpox, yellow fever, malaria, bubonic plague, typhoid fever, poliomyelitis, diphtheria, influenza, or tuberculosis—not when they attempt to cure these diseases.

There are some troublesome diseases that doctors do not yet know how to prevent effectively—mental retardation, coronary heart disease, arthritis, mental disease, and cancer. They would be at least partially successful, however, in these cases if they paid more attention to the quality of the internal environments of their patients. The cells and tissues within our bodies are not likely to malfunction if we give them —by well-balanced nutrition—an excellent environment in which to live.

Legal restrictions appropriately prevent biochemists from testing and experimenting with human beings. We do, however, perform certain experiments with animals. We have, for example, tested the hypothesis that an excellent internal environment will prevent disease. We chose as a test case the development of cataracts in the eyes of young rats known to be caused by too much galactose in the rats' diets. (Galactose is a simple sugar derived from lactose, milk sugar.) No one had been able to prevent this disease, but we were successful on our first trial.

Forty-eight young rats were *all* given diets in which twenty percent of the calories were in the form of galactose. For twenty-four of these rats, the diets and their resulting internal environments were of mediocre quality—and the results were poor. Every one of the twenty-four rats developed at least one cataract; twenty-three of the twenty-four developed cataracts in *both eyes.*

Although we gave the other twenty-four rats the same amount of galactose, we also gave them an excellent assortment of all the nutrient chemicals young rats need. These rats thus had an excellent internal environment. The results were surprisingly dramatic. Not a single rat developed a cataract in either eye. We had prevented the disease completely!

This was an important test case. The indications are

that we could also prevent human cataracts if we had the expertise to provide the human subjects with *excellent* internal environments. Medical scientists, amazingly, have never tried out this type of prevention on human cataracts. Furthermore, on the basis of this test case, we may presume that we could prevent many other serious conditions, including alcoholism, by developing excellent internal environments in the threatened subject.

Prevention is vastly more economical than treatment. Disease prevention decreases human suffering. All the facts endorse prevention and nothing is against it. It is the only sensible course.

10

How Much Would
Prevention of Alcoholism
Be Worth?

You can probably answer the following questions for yourself: How much would it be worth to me as an individual to avoid alcoholism? Each person will have a different answer.

If you are *sure* that alcoholism can never happen to you (and how can you be sure?), then it would be worth nothing. However, on the off chance that you may drift into this trouble, prevention should be a high priority with you because of the terrible effects of this disease. The inner conflicts it spawns, the torture of frustrations that accompany the disease, its tenacity, its hopelessness, and its devastating effects on all human relationships make alcoholism one of the worst possible maladies. The fact that it insidiously creeps up on the unwary should cause concern in everyone.

Each person must answer this question for himself or herself: How important is it for me to build and protect my internal environment and thus avoid irreparable damage?

Is prevention of alcoholism worth the trouble of protecting my internal environment? For the sake of the members of my family for whom I care and who care for me, is it something I want to do? Improvement of one's internal environment can completely turn around his or her whole attitude toward life, emotions, and hopes for the future. Is this worth considering?

Alcoholism, if you allow it to develop and go unchecked, can literally ruin every single aspect of your life. Think of the psychological boost it will give you as an individual to know that you, by your own initiative and efforts, can meet this problem head-on and thus avoid the needless torture of alcohol addiction. You can then hold up your head and be proud of your membership in the human race.

If this is worthwhile for you as an individual, think of its value to society. Multiply the benefit to you by however many millions there are who also will accept and follow the commonsense idea that a stitch in time will save 99,999!

The quantity of loss of life that can be directly attributed to alcoholism is of great magnitude. According to figures released by the National Council on Alcoholism, thirty-one percent of all suicides are alcoholics. The suicide rate among alcoholics is fifty-eight times that of nonalcoholics.

Fifty percent of all fatal automobile accidents involve alcohol. The yearly fatality rate is forty thousand to fifty thousand per year, so the toll attributable to excessive use of alcohol may be twenty thousand per year. The Vietnam War, in which the United States was involved from 1961 to 1974, is generally considered a disaster, and indeed it was. The total loss of American lives was approximately fifty-six thousand. During those same thirteen years, automobile accidents caused the deaths of twelve times that number, and if the excessive use of alcohol was to blame for half the automobile deaths, the yearly toll from this cause is six times that of the yearly death toll of the Vietnam War. And it goes on and on. No ceasefire will discontinue the highway carnage. In addition to those killed yearly in traffic accidents, another two million persons are injured. A substantial part of all crime also is alcohol related.

How much does alcoholism cost our economy? If

we could eliminate alcoholism from our current population and prevent its recurrence, this would save us at least $25 billion a year. Some estimates are much higher than this.

Considering the economic aspects alone, I regard this book as a multi-billion dollar project. If we can save even ten percent of those who presently lean toward alcoholism, this would mean a saving to industry of *at least* $2.5 billion a year. We should save a much higher percentage if this book is taken seriously. If we do not, it will be a poor reflection on our intelligence and the effectiveness of education.

At the present time at least thirty million young people and adults in this country are in some danger of eventually becoming alcoholics. As the ten million who are currently alcoholics die off (their death rate is much higher than the average) there will be, according to present trends, more than ten million to take their places—persons who are not now alcoholics.

Think what would happen if the millions who are not now alcoholics could continue to maintain their will power and "won't power," take good care of themselves, and stay out of the ranks of alcoholics. We would have eliminated one of the most terrible and threatening diseases of mankind! We would have saved millions of heartbreaks, prevented the disintegration of millions of families, and provided safety for millions of children.

Abraham Lincoln, in a speech to a Women's Christian Temperance Union (WCTU) meeting February 22, 1848, made the following statement: "If we take habitual drunkards as a class, their heads and hearts will bear an advantageous comparison to any other class. There seems ever to be a proneness to this vice among the brilliant and warmhearted. The demon of intemperance seems ever to delight in sucking the blood of genius and generosity."

Lincoln was not alone in observing that alcoholism often strikes unusually able people. If this observation is valid, society loses an inordinate amount of able talent when alcoholism is as rampant as it is today.

The strategy we present in this book can prevent the loss of these able people. Able people are more likely to be receptive than average people to the advantages of thoroughgoing health education.

In studies of the economics of alcoholism, we find that while many problem drinkers have no jobs and are in the lower socio-economic stratum, often it has been their drinking problem that has caused the sorry state of their economic affairs.

It saddens me greatly to think of the growing problem of alcoholism among teenagers. Currently it is estimated that there are 3.3 million youngsters fourteen to seventeen years old who suffer from a variety of alcohol related problems. Our schools and homes should teach them that they possess inborn individuality; we should instruct them about the importance of their internal environments and the hidden chemicals necessary for health. We should stop telling them, by example and in advertising, that "important" people drink freely.

We do not prepare youngsters to cope with the problem of alcoholism, and we are being hypocritical when we blame them for wanting to be like adults and wanting to emulate prominent and prosperous members of the adult population.

In an interview, one young college girl says:

"I drink a heck of a lot, but I know that I'm not in any deep trouble and I'm in no way an alcoholic.... Lots of times I drive when I'm drinking. I can drive just as good.... I've gotten totally wasted every night of this summer and had a great time, too. I'm sure my liver is also wasted, but I've had a blast. Every morning I tell myself that I won't ever drink again, but then, that same night, I go do it again."

It is obvious to *me* that this girl is already in serious trouble though she is blithely sure she is not.

For more than twenty-five years I have been urging attendance to the nutritional aspects of alcoholism. While there is a current growing interest, it is belated, and only now is the importance of nutrition percolating into the minds of the opinion makers who talk the most about alcoholism. Years ago Mark Twain said, "The man with the new idea is a crank until the idea succeeds."

If what I am saying makes sense to you, my readers, you can help make the percentage saved from alcoholism much higher than it would be otherwise, by speaking out to your friends, your neighbors, physicians, psychiatrists, "experts" on alcoholism, and promoters of "alcohol programs," for which you pay through contributions and taxes.

Victor Hugo wrote, "There is one thing stronger than all the armies in the world and that is an idea whose time has come."

The time is come to prevent alcoholism.

Eventually is too late. Why not now?

Part III

Alcoholism as an "Alien Disease"

11

How I Became Interested in the Alcoholism Problem

In 1946, after long deliberation and study, I wrote *The Human Frontier* (Harcourt, Brace), a revelation of man's individuality. Briefly stated, the fundamental idea was this: In order to progress and solve our problems we need to understand *real people*, who *as individuals* are entirely different from hypothetical "man" with whom poets and philosophers often concern themselves.

Although the book enjoyed a substantial sale and *Reader's Digest* published a review of it in many languages, most readers regarded it as a passing curiosity and failed to grasp its real import. Wasn't it funny, they thought, that some people have such interesting peculiarities?

One person who did recognize the importance of the book's content was a prominent, nationally known sociologist, Professor Samuel Stouffer of Harvard University. I vividly remember a conversation with him in Washington in 1946 in which he told me, "Thirty years from now *The Human Frontier* will be looked upon as an epoch-making book." This pleased me, of course—he evidently recognized that the ideas were universal in their application—but I wondered, "Why *thirty* years?"

Twenty-five years later I published an article, "The Biology of Behavior," in *Saturday Review*, which addressed again the theme of *The Human Frontier*. As a result of this publication, I received eighteen separate requests for permission to reprint the entire article in various books and magazines. Evidently this basic idea, by now, was attractive enough to stir a great deal of interest.

Working on *The Human Frontier* convinced me that individuals are in many respects so inherently different from each other that without an understanding of these differences many *serious* problems arise and persist.

When *The Human Frontier* was off the press, I turned back to my professional work as a biochemist and asked myself: In light of my special insight into the importance of inborn individuality, to what human problem can I address myself to make the largest contribution? I thought of accident proneness as a possible area for study—also the problems of marriage or divorce. But then I thought of alcoholism. Reading everything pertinent on the subject convinced me that here was a human problem crying for solution—a problem that no one could solve without a basic understanding of how people differ from each other in their fundamental physiology and biochemistry.

In 1947 I published an extensive and comprehensive article on the etiology, or root causes, of alcoholism, my first publication on the subject. At the time this article was written, A. J. Carlson, the famous physiologist and head of a National Committee on Alcoholism, said it was the best thing that had ever been written on the subject.

I questioned the notion, current at the time, and current today, that a person's environment, i.e., external environment, was the most significant cause of alcohol addiction. My questioning revolved around this issue: Were the environmental difficulties of the alcoholic-to-be any greater than those of a person who resisted alcoholism?

Thus emerged the idea that alcoholism is indeed an environmental problem—but an "inner environmental" problem, linked to a person's individuality.

It was in that 1947 paper that I first wrote a working hypothesis of alcoholism: Environmental factors are potent and indispensable for bringing about alcoholism, but they do not do so unless the person involved possesses the type of metabolic individuality that predisposes toward addiction.

I approached the subject broadly, left every avenue open, but stressed the importance of the physiological area with which I was most familiar. I also stressed, on the basis of extensive material I presented in *The Human Frontier*, that some individuals are far more susceptible to disease than others. Investigators in the field of alcoholism have never accepted, digested, and tested this idea. It is, in my opinion, a cornerstone idea which medical science can no longer reject.

12

A Note for Those Concerned with Confirmed Alcoholics

Preventing alcoholism with the measures I suggest is relatively simple and direct. In spite of the simplicity of the principles involved in prevention, the treatment of actual alcoholics remains a substantial medical problem that lies outside the domain of this book. This book deals with prevention—the only sensible long-range approach to the problem.

Alcoholics, sooner or later, perhaps early and often, come under the care of medical doctors in some hospital or sanitarium. Physicians are often experienced and competent in dealing with the sobering-up process; but unless they can do something more than sober up a person, the fundamental, untreated problem still exists. Most likely the alcoholic will be back in the hospital again and again, possibly dozens of times.

From my point of view, above all else, we need to raise the quality of the internal environment of the alcoholic from a low level up to a respectable level. A bad internal environment is self-perpetuating and seriously affects all normal body and brain activities. To improve an alcoholic's inner environment, he must not only eliminate alcohol, but he must supply his body, through good food and otherwise, with the approximately forty hidden chemicals so that rebuilding can take place.

My book, *Alcoholism: The Nutritional Approach* (1959), was written to help alcoholics recover their physiological equilibrium by building up their internal environments. It has helped thousands of members of Alcoholics Anonymous and others to learn to live with satisfaction and pleasure without alcohol. The writing of this book was a public service venture. I attempted to give all the royalties from the book to Alcoholics Anonymous to whom I dedicated it, but Alcoholics Anonymous receives no contributions from "outsiders," so I gave the royalties to the National Council on Alcoholism.

This book has influenced and helped many thousands of people who have written me letters of appreciation. It has gained particular notice in recent years. The University of Texas Press has published not only the hardback edition but also three paperback editions. They have recently released a ninth printing.

Physicians who let this book influence them pay increasingly more attention to the nutritional status of the alcoholics who come under their care. This is particularly true of the physicians who are members of, or sympathetic with, the Academy of Orthomolecular Psychiatry, the International Academy of Preventive Medicine, the International College of Applied Nutrition, and similar organizations.

As a result of progress in disseminating information about the nutritional approach, many physicians who deal with alcoholics are aware of the importance of nutrition in treating alcoholic patients even though their knowledge may be fragmentary.

Some physicians with broad experience have had considerable success using "megavitamin therapy" in the treatment of alcoholics. As they extend and refine these treatments we may expect more dramatic benefits. Many members of Alcoholics Anonymous state with conviction that specific nutrients are effective in curbing their craving for liquor.

Some physicians, doing work unrelated to alcoholism, have centered their interest in recent years on a procedure called "hyperalimentation." Intravenous feeding, traditionally, has meant the continuous intravenous supply of glucose, especially to surgical patients. This idea has expanded into the use of a more complete mixture of nutrients. One of the leaders in the use of hyperalimentation is Dr. Stanley J. Dudrick, chairman of surgery at the University of Texas Medical School in Houston. He predicts that before too long every person entering a hospital will receive a nutrition analysis as routinely as one now receives blood and urine tests.

Physicians—and no others—are in a position to administer nutrients by injection, and some are making comprehensive efforts to improve the whole internal environment by this means. This is a most worthy objective, and alcoholic patients should often have the advantage of this treatment. Of course, doctors need expertise in this area; inadequate planning of procedures may yield dubious results.

I am sure that hyperalimentation is a coming treatment for alcoholics and for others with metabolic problems. Experienced doctors in the field of alcoholism tell me that a patient who is merely "dried out" is a sad specimen compared to one whom they "dry out" and also provide adequate nutritional attention.

Adequate nutritional attention spells R-E-H-A-B-I-L-I-T-A-T-I-O-N.

13

Why Does the
Medical Profession
Look Upon Alcoholism as
an "Alien Disease"?

It is a well-known fact that physicians in general, including specialists in internal medicine and in psychiatry, usually do not wish to have victims of alcoholism as patients. Severe cases are given temporary treatment, often in mental hospitals, but the sobering up process is not designed to correct the fundamental disease that brought them to the hospital. Very commonly, physicians refer severe cases to Alcoholics Anonymous, a group with alcoholism experience but usually with no training whatever in medicine, psychiatry, physiology, or biochemistry. This is treating alcoholism like an "alien" or "outlaw" disease.

There are reasons why physicians deal with alcoholism entirely differently than they do with other outstandingly important diseases. The reasons, as we shall see, are numerous and extremely complex. They are based upon (1) the unusual nature of the disease, (2) limitations in the fundamental strategy of medical research, (3) human nature and psychology, (4) professional psychology, (5) the kind of education we all receive in school, (6) the kind of training physicians receive in medical schools, and (7) the kind of ideas that are commonly afloat in our society.

In the succeeding eight chapters of this book I will

discuss these reasons, and I believe the reader will agree that these are realistic reasons and that the deficiencies of the medical profession with respect to alcoholism are the result of neither consistent stupidity nor a villainous plot.

14

Alcoholism Is an Insidious, Creeping Disease, Extremely Difficult to Diagnose

A prominent public official divorced his wife; the reason the official gave for the breakup of his marriage was his wife's "alcoholism." This stunned their friends and family alike. The wife was a joyous, fun-loving young woman, who did take a drink now and then. To her straitlaced husband, this was "alcoholism."

Alcoholism is difficult to diagnose because of its relation to value systems, to morality, and to social life generally. Physicians find the puzzle of alcoholism even more confounding because there is no known clinical test to determine its existence. If "everybody" says that "so and so" is an alcoholic, this may satisfy some, but gossip, hearsay, and inexpert testimony and opinion are poor substitutes for objective and verifiable evidence. The lack of a clinical test for alcoholism is one of the many reasons why medical science has moved so slowly in the field.

Another diagnostic difficulty rests upon the fact that alcoholism is truly a creeping disease. The precise point at which it becomes overt alcoholism is difficult, even impossible, to determine. A person may have slight difficulty turning down additional drinks long before his or her drinking becomes compulsive. This book on the prevention of alcoholism is directed primarily to those who are beginning to have slight difficulties in control. For some, loss of control comes very, very slowly; for others, it may come more rapidly. In every case alcoholism is a progressive disease and the victim has some time in which to apply preventive measures. For the purpose of prevention, nothing can take the place of self-diagnosis. For a person incapable of perceiving that control is slipping, there is small hope for prevention.

Another important characteristic of alcoholism, which makes it difficult for medical science to master, is that the disease involves a type of pathology that medical science has not heretofore recognized—generalized *cytopathy*, or cell sickness.

In *Physicians' Handbook of Nutritional Science* (Charles C Thomas, 1975), I presented for the first time this novel concept of pathology. When crucial nutrients —essential to every cell in the body—are lacking or are in short supply, damage occurs in every cell in the body. This may impair any and every bodily function to a greater or lesser extent. In terms of the generalized cytopathy concept, then, alcoholism is in every case not only a brain disease but also, in varying degrees, a disease of the liver and of every other organ and tissue.

Traditionally, medical scientists consider pathology as localized. They study and catalogue pathological conditions on the basis of where lesions occur—here, there, or elsewhere. Alcoholism does not fit at all into this picture. It is a disease in which everything goes wrong and a diagnostician cannot spot any single lesion indicative of the disease.

Medical schools do not train pathologists so that they recognize generalized cytopathy. In this condition, more diffuse than most pathologies, the whole community of organs, tissues, and cells suffers from internal (biochemical) impairment even though the organs, tissues, and cells limp along and remain alive. Alcoholism is such a disease. It is something like aging, in that it most certainly impairs all healthy activity and ultimately causes death, yet it attacks no single tissue or organ to the exclusion of others. Doctors, therefore, cannot point their finger to any spot in the body that is diagnostically significant.

15

Alcoholism Is a
Metabolic Disease

No one who has studied alcoholism can challenge the statement that alcoholism is a metabolic disease—i.e., a derangement of the biochemical machinery of the body. When a person consumes alcohol it definitely enters into his or her metabolic process; when one consumes it in excess, it may greatly alter the whole metabolic scheme of operation. The metabolic nature of alcoholism is an important reason for lack of progress in eradicating the trouble. Medical scientists in this period of medical history find major metabolic diseases difficult, if not impossible, to understand and manage satisfactorily.

Many baffling diseases—mental disease, circulatory disease, renal disease, muscular dystrophy, multiple sclerosis, cystic fibrosis, and cancer—have extremely important roots in tissue and cellular metabolism. Their complexity makes these diseases baffling to everybody, but metabolic experts have the best chance of making progress with them.

The study of metabolism is particularly exacting because a knowledge of general chemistry, organic chemistry, and physical chemistry as well as bio-chemistry, biology, and genetics is basic. Few investigators indeed have a working understanding of what takes place in metabolism.

A chart hanging on the wall of my office reminds me daily of the complexity of metabolism. This chart, covered with relatively fine print, is about three by five feet in size and presents in abbreviated form much that is presently known about metabolism. When the study of metabolism was in its infancy just a few decades ago, a small chart on a single page of a textbook covered the then current knowledge on this subject.

The current chart presents the names or formulas of an estimated 3,000 metabolic substances (metabolites) along with their interrelationships. It also gives the names of the enzymes (about 1,100 in number) that bring about the transformations occurring in metabolism. Biochemists have isolated and purified virtually all the metabolites and enzymes this chart designates.

The study of metabolism continues to expand rapidly and its complexity keeps increasing. Subsequent metabolic charts will have to be significantly larger and more complicated. It is not uncommon for a biochemist to spend a lifetime of study clarifying only one tiny segment of a metabolic chart. It is safe to say that the metabolism taking place in our bodies involves *thousands* of enzymes and a corresponding number of chemical transformations. These take place every minute and every second of our lives. Our bodies are certainly as complex as a big city with its thousands of factories, businesses, and services.

The metabolic chart in my office tells only a small part of the story. It fails to give information about the distinctive metabolism of any individual person. It indicates various "cycles" and "pathways of metabolism," but it does not provide information regarding the relative prevalence of these cycles and pathways in different tissues and in different persons.

To ascertain how an individual's peculiarities in metabolism may increase his or her susceptibility to alcoholism can be a mind-boggling endeavor. In the light of this fact the limited progress in the study of alcoholism as a metabolic disease is understandable.

A lack of clear-cut and compelling objectives on the part of investigators further compounds the difficulties of studying alcoholism in a commonsense manner. I shall have more to say on this later. Studying the metabolic aspects of alcoholism cannot be simple, but it is not hopeless.

16

The Conspicuous Lack of Comprehensive Disease-Oriented Research Institutions

Western countries have not promoted the establishment of a series of disease-oriented medical institutes that would each center its attention on the comprehensive (multidisciplinary) study of a particular disease. This failure to develop broad approaches to the study of different diseases has led to serious and costly deficiencies in research, and, in my opinion, a heartbreaking delay in eliminating some diseases.

A research institute dedicated to the comprehensive exploration of coronary heart disease, for example, should most certainly concern itself with broad and deep questions such as, "What role does heredity play?" "How does psychology enter in?" And "How does nutrition fit into the picture?" But unfortunately, up until the last decade no such institute existed and no one was inclined to look at the problem in a comprehensive way. While the word *nutrition* appeared in the literature of the National Heart and Lung Institute, no in-depth study of nutrition was involved, as I found out when I was a member of the President's Panel on Heart Disease in 1972. The material presented in chapter 21 of this book was at that time unrecognized.

Although I have not had recent direct contact with

the National Institute of Arthritis and Metabolic Disease, the National Institute of Mental Health, or the National Cancer Institute, etc., I have followed nutritional advances carefully and know that there has been no serious revolution in the attitude toward nutrition. Historically these institutes and the medical profession generally have approached problems related to nutrition in an unsatisfactory way, but I cannot offer substantive proof. All medical research has suffered from the lack of coordinated disease-oriented approaches. Nutrition is not the only neglected phase.

Genetics has often received scant consideration and the role of psychology in other than mental diseases has been inadequately explored.

Multidisciplinary studies go against the grain in all universities because of their compartmentalization. It is practically impossible to get approval and financial support for any study involving, for example, biochemistry, genetics, and psychology. To get such support would require approval by three panels of experts and the chances of getting such approval would be infinitesimally small.

One of the main reasons medical progress in the field of alcoholism has been so slow is that in decades past it has been nobody's business to study alcoholism comprehensively in a multidisciplinary way.

The 1976 Rand Report,* though it is meritorious in some respects, is also a reflection on the past history of alcoholism research because it gives very little importance to the role of nutrition in the problem of alcoholism.

The International Bureau Against Alcoholism in 1963 published a sixty-three-page *Handbook of Organizations*** operating in eighteen countries, providing a review of the pertinent research activities of each. Fifteen such organizations are working in the United States, three in France, two each in Canada, Czechoslovakia, Finland, Australia, Hungary, Italy, and one each in Great Britain, Denmark, Belgium, the Union

*See Appendix III, Addendum, Ref. 4.
**See Appendix III, Addendum, Ref. 2.

of Soviet Socialist Republics, Switzerland, the Netherlands, Chile, Norway, Thailand, and Sweden.

A perusal of this handbook leads to several observations: (1) Many of the organizations include much in addition to alcoholism research; (2) treatment, not prevention, of alcoholism is a dominant theme; (3) the vast majority of organizations are psychiatrically or sociologically oriented; (4) those organizations that deal with metabolism are primarily academically oriented and exhibit little or no direct interest in the question of how alcoholism-prone individuals differ in their metabolism from alcoholism-resistant individuals; (5) the handbook rarely considers, even by implication, the question of whether, or to what extent, nutrition relates to alcoholism. The work of the Alcohol Monopoly in Finland is, however, better balanced than most.

In our country, the Yale Center for Alcohol Studies exhibited substantial world leadership from its inception in 1944 up until 1962. At that time Rutgers University sponsored the continuation of this effort. Unfortunately, their efforts cultivated only a psychological and sociological approach, leaving biochemistry, metabolism, and prevention out in the cold.

Comprehensive study is mandatory in the case of every major disease—*mental retardation, coronary heart disease, arthritis, mental disease, alcoholism,* and *cancer.* This involves asking numerous questions with respect to each. In the past decade many of these questions have gone unanswered or have been considered in a superficial way. How does psychology come into play? How is endocrinology involved? Do inborn anatomical discordances enter? Do inborn metabolic factors play a role? How is nutrition implicated?

It is difficult to accept the fact that no well-supported laboratory or institute exists that devotes itself to the thorough investigation of the question: How is cancer related to nutrition? It is correspondingly difficult for me to accept the fact that no well-supported institute studies the relation between nutrition and alcoholism.

What our culture sorely needs is many broad-gauged scientists interested in the challenge of exploring alcoholism and other major diseases *thoroughly*. When we can produce such scientists in abundance we can make many giant strides for mankind in conquering or preventing baffling maladies.

17

Human (and Medical)
Resistance to New Ideas

Another one of the reasons for lack of progress toward the elimination of alcoholism is the natural tendency we human beings have to defend traditional ideas and reject anything that sounds new and different. Inertia guides us to reject *new* ideas in all areas—in law, politics, commerce, religion, and even in science. This reluctance to accept new ideas has value; many new ideas are screwy and we must scrutinize all of them before accepting any.

It is not surprising, then, that physicians tend to adhere to time-honored ideas even after the ideas cry for revision.

An idea that has had a profound retarding effect on progress in the study of alcoholism is that it is a *psychiatric disease*. Let's scrutinize this notion. Of course there is something wrong with an alcoholic's psyche, but the trouble probably has its roots in aberrant brain *metabolism*. Alcoholism is not primarily of psychogenic origin—caused by wrong thinking. Clearly, alcohol interacting with a susceptible individual causes it. Alcoholism is a psychiatric disease, but it is also a physiological, biochemical, and metabolic disease. This being the case, those who consider it from the purely psychological viewpoint are not grasping the complete picture. Alcoholics should not be the responsibility solely of psychiatrists. The entire medical profession should be responsible for their rehabilitation and well-being.

Another time-honored idea that has retarded progress with respect to alcoholism is that *physicians deal with sickness*. That is, of course, literally true, but it is far from the whole truth. Physicians deal also with health. In fact, some physicians, as well as those outside the profession, believe physicians' greatest responsibility is to help keep people well. It is said that some cultures punish medicine men when their "patients" become ill. Such a policy would be a powerful incentive for preventive medicine.

Many people accept the philosophy that in effect advises people, "Get sick first, then we will take care of you." Alcoholics Anonymous has, in effect, adopted this idea. With goodwill, not malice, it says to those having trouble with alcohol, "If you become an alcoholic, confess it, then we will do for you what we can."

The prevention of alcoholism—the only sensible way to deal with the problem—is in direct conflict with the disease-oriented approach to medicine.

Another well-grounded idea that deters progress in the battle with alcoholism is: *Doctors use medicines to treat and cure disease*. Again, this is literally true, but it is only a part of the truth. Unfortunately, the use of medicines (most often agents foreign to the human body) plays an enormous role in modern medicine and this discourages to an alarming extent the use of natural chemicals (normally present in our bodies) to prevent disease. I treated this subject extensively in the book, *Nutrition Against Disease*.

No known *medicine* will successfully treat or cure alcoholism, and I believe we never will discover such a medicine. The best treatment is the preventive measure of furnishing the cells in the patient's body and brain a completely adequate environment. Searching for medicines as a substitute is futile.

When time-honored ideas and our vested interests coincide, we tenaciously protect these ideas. Because their training has been in the direction of using medicines, physicians hesitate to de-emphasize medicines.

The pharmaceutical industry, with its tremendous economic stake, works assiduously on members of the medical profession—even during the training of physicians—to perpetuate the idea that a physician's prime duty is to treat sick people with appropriate medicines and drugs.

When Louis Pasteur, a chemist, not a physician, advanced the idea about one hundred years ago that *infective agents (such as bacteria) produce disease*, the medical profession met the idea with scorn and terrific resistance. Eventually, however, the evidence became incontrovertible. The medical profession recognized Pasteur as a genius and accepted wholeheartedly and enthusiastically the "theory" that microorganisms cause disease.

This acceptance was phenomenally productive and desirable. Physicians may have accepted the idea too fully, however. There has since been some tendency to assume that infective agents cause almost every disease.

An example of this assumption is the assignment the Dutch government gave Dr. Eijkman in 1886 when it sent him to Java to "identify the microorganism that was causing beriberi." In 1897 Dr. Eijkman published the results of his famous experiment in which chickens fed only polished rice developed polyneuritis (the fowl counterpart of beriberi). Eating the rice polishings cured the chickens. Even his own experiment did not convince Dr. Eijkman. He and others were reluctant to recognize and admit that microorganisms did not cause the disease. It was not until 1929 that he received the Nobel prize in medicine for his work on beriberi. I have a deep-seated confidence in the intelligence of the medical profession and its ability to discover ultimate truths.

Another progress-delaying idea with respect to alcoholism is that *nutrition is a field for quacks and charlatans*. Physicians by the tens of thousands still tell their patients, "All you have to do is to eat a balanced diet." Literally this may be true; but most often those who give this advice have no real grasp of what a "balanced diet" means. They neither know nor appreciate that there are approximately forty hidden chemicals that are necessary for this balance and that many energy-yielding foods, such as sugar, alcohol, white rice, white flour products, tend to *un*balance diets. They are unaware that it is difficult for individuals to acquire from their external environment the balance they need to provide an excellent internal environment for their cells and tissues.

Why are physicians usually "turned off" when the subject of nutrition comes up? One reason is that medical schools develop this negative attitude. Again it is pertinent to ask: Why?

Medical schools teach students to be critical and careful. Enthusiasts and quacks who ignorantly make unwarranted claims have long plagued medical science and scientific nutrition, and thus have given nutrition a bad name.

Another factor making physicians doubtful about nutrition is that qualified scientists outside the medical profession rather than those within medicine have made many of the significant advances. Medical educators have been slow to accept and make use of these advances.

Many persons mistakenly think of vitamins as "medicines"—medicines that laymen may utilize without the help of physicians. Thus, many physicians are reluctant to mention vitamins or use them in their practice. Only in recent years has this begun to change.

Because medical schools have neglected nutrition, doctors often are unaware that vitamins (as well as essential minerals and amino acids) are not medicines or drugs at all. They are nutrients and act constructively and cooperatively to strengthen our life machinery and make metabolism possible. Medicines (drugs) do not do this. Drugs often make us feel better by interfering with certain aspects of metabolism in such a way as to yield seemingly favorable results. Antibiotics do so by interfering with the metabolism of invading organisms.

18

Medical Emphasis on Cure and Treatment Rather Than Prevention

Prevention of infectious diseases has developed in a remarkable and most commendable fashion. Medical science controls some of these diseases, such as smallpox, yellow fever, and bubonic plague, so well that from a practical standpoint we almost forget they exist.

Physicians *treat* certain diseases but fail to prevent them. Public health experts are, generally speaking, sympathetic to the idea of prevention but they are outside the mainstream of medicine. Many medical scientists think very little about disease prevention.

The principal reason for this neglect is that many diseases are metabolic in nature. The intricacies of metabolism remain a mind-boggling mystery to all but a few biochemists who may feel relatively at home in the area.

Another reason for this neglect is the increasing influence of the pharmaceutical industry, which continually invents and promotes new drugs or medicines. This industry effectively propagandizes physicians, who then prescribe their drugs. These interests would, if they could, transform the field of "medicine" into the field of "medicines."

Medicines are not preventive agents. When doctors

use them to the exclusion of preventive agents, prevention, as an aim, has gone out the window.

Notwithstanding the fact that the policy of *preventing* alcoholism stands in strong contrast to the policy of treating alcoholism after it strikes, the medical profession is, to a high degree, treatment-oriented and medicine-oriented. Physicians in general are not yet moving rapidly in the direction of prevention. Usually they "wait to see what happens."

Times are changing, however, and prevention is on the way.

19

Tunnel Vision and Extreme Specialization

Some individuals' eyes are built with poor peripheral vision, so that they have in effect "tunnel vision." This occurs in differing degrees. If peripheral vision is almost totally lacking, the tunnel vision is extreme; if, on the other hand, peripheral vision is only slightly impaired, the tunnel vision may be slight. Diminished peripheral vision prevents a broad view. One can see what is straight ahead but relatively little that is to the right or the left.

Correspondingly, some minds have the same trait; they operate in a narrow range and tend not to see anything in broad perspective.

In the days when all medical practice was general practice, the medical profession attracted those with broad interests and wide-ranging capabilities. In these days, however, when there is so much specialization in medical practice, persons with limited interests often go into the profession.

For reasons I have already discussed, alcoholism is not a disease that specialists with narrow interests can successfully attack. The diseased condition probably involves every cell in the body, and it certainly affects every human activity.

Those outside the medical profession who have turned their attention to alcoholism have exhibited "tunnel vision" to an alarming and disconcerting degree. The opinion makers in the field of alcoholism in the past have often accepted the view that alcoholism is a disease with psychic origin and have centered their "tunnel vision" on this aspect.

Fourteen years ago I wrote an article, "Alcoholism Is Like an Elephant," to emphasize the need to look at alcoholism from *all* angles. Since the opinion makers at that time did not accept this idea with open arms—they preferred their "tunnel vision" approach—publication of the article did not take place. I present this article here in its entirety.

Alcoholism Is Like an Elephant

Alcoholism is like an elephant. What it resembles depends on how one approaches it, especially if one is Mr. Magoo and extremely shortsighted. Approaching a leg, the elephant becomes a tree; the tail suggests a rope; the trunk a huge snake. To sociologists alcoholism is something associated with special social conditions; to psychologists it is a manifestation of a disordered mind; physiologists and biochemists are likely to think of it in terms of a disordered physiology or biochemistry.

The writer is anxious that the Magoo analysis of alcoholism be abandoned. Sociology, psychology, physiology, and biochemistry *all* come into play and are thoroughly intertwined. Alcoholism is a *human* disease, and we human beings are not built in compartments, each of which can be sick or well, independent of the others. We need to look at the whole elephant, not one or two isolated parts.

A long admirer of AA, the writer appreciates not only its practical achievements in helping alcoholics but also its basic philosophy, which is good for everyone, whether they are alcoholics or not. Because of my special interest in biochemical individuality, I have an extremely high regard for the AA prayer, which is unique in that it recognizes "things I cannot change" and pleads for wisdom to know the difference between what can be changed and what cannot. This wisdom does not come easily, and one of the prime objectives of my life is to make possible an increase in this kind of wisdom. It is my conviction that the very same problem enters the lives of each of us whether alcoholic or not; we need wisdom to recognize and cultivate our best potentialities and the maturity and humility to know that we have shortcomings. These considerations force us to live *our own* lives.

There are many who will give lip service—even *ardent* lip service—to the idea of looking at the whole elephant but will then proceed to talk and write blithely and endlessly, forgetting all about the physiological and biochemical aspects of alcoholism. There are those who think that "research" on alcoholism can move along quite satisfactorily leaving out physiology and biochemistry. These are a special type of Mr. Magoo.

There are some highly important considerations implied but not made explicit in the well-known AA twelve steps suggested as a program of recovery. It is obvious, but not stated, that an alcoholic will, in the course of his attempt to recover, be expected to *eat food*. To one who looks only at certain parts of the elephant, this seems like an unimportant detail, but to one who has devoted a lifetime of study to the biochemistry of nutrition, this is worth serious attention —along with the other aspects.

Will improved social conditions help an alcoholic to recover? My answer is "Yes." Will improved psychological conditions and spiritual attitudes help? My answer is "Yes." Will an improved physiological and biochemical environment speed his recovery? My answer is "Yes."

Sanitation and shelter may be taken for granted; exercise and sleep may be more important than we think. But one part of our environment that is highly variable and under our control—the food we eat— demands far more attention on the part of alcoholics *and others* than it gets. When a small baby cries, it is likely that food is needed, and we know that *what* we feed the baby makes a difference. At what stage in our lives does what we eat cease to make a difference? Never! This is true whether we are alcoholics or not.

In a book dedicated to Alcoholics Anonymous I have sought to tell how nutrition can help an alcoholic recover, and how, if properly applied, it can prevent the disease from developing. When one goes to a physician, one of the first things the physician should be concerned about is whether or not the patient is getting the *right amounts* of the forty or more nutritional *essentials*—amino acids, vitamins, minerals—that everyone of us needs. This problem needs to be approached in an expert way, but unfortunately most physicians are not nutritional experts and this aspect usually receives only step-motherly attention. Recently it has been discovered that one type of feeble-mindedness can be prevented by changing the diet of the threatened youngster, and it is hoped that this advance will help awaken more interest in the nutritional approach to many other diseases. This particular change in diet was a sophisticated one—putting the small child on a diet nearly free from one of the essential amino acids—phenylalanine—and was far more intricate and exacting, for instance, than merely changing from one baby food formula to another.

It is my conviction after over fifteen years of study, at the level of an expert, that proper nutrition on a sophisticated level and with due recognition that we have a high degree of individuality in our body chemistries, can help alcoholics tremendously in their attempts to recover and can prevent alcoholism from developing. The uniqueness of the body chemistry of each of us is a *fact*, not a theory. The nutritional phase is a part of the "elephant" that has not been duly considered. I would not subtract the tiniest bit from what anyone has done or can do to help alcoholics by psychological or spiritual counseling. I would merely add another tool, one that, in my judgment, will prove highly effective.

20

Failure to Recognize Inborn Individuality as a Crucial Factor

In the six preceding chapters of this book I have discussed important reasons why the medical profession fails to make fundamental progress in dealing with alcoholism. I have left, however, two of the most pertinent and far-reaching reasons for this and the following chapter.

Having spent almost thirty years of my scientific life studying inborn individuality, while others have paid little attention to it, I admit to having an unusual point of view. But, on the basis of extensive study and thought, I believe firmly that so long as we leave inborn individuality out of the alcoholism picture our understanding of the disease will remain foggy and our ability to deal with it in a reliable way will remain seriously impaired.

Only *individuals* become alcoholics. This disease does not attack families, social clubs, towns, cities, states, or countries. It attacks individuals within such groups. Practically speaking, alcohol does things to some people it doesn't do to others. We need to know why. The alcohol is the same; the individuals are different. What is it that makes some individuals highly resistant? We need to know the answer to this question, and we cannot find it out by concentrating on average or hypothetical people. We need to gather pertinent data from individual people.

There is abundant room for investigation, but researchers have done precious little. What inborn differences might give us clues as to why individual persons react so differently to alcohol? Substantial and often very large inborn differences exist in fundamental metabolism, in gross anatomy, in microscopic anatomy, in endocrinology, in the composition of body tissues and body fluids, in excretion patterns, in secretion patterns, in enzyme levels, in the physiological and psychic responses to chemicals that are natural to our bodies, in the physiological and psychic responses to alcohol and to chemicals that are foreign to our bodies, in the sensory systems, and in nutritional needs.

The broad metabolic field offers major promise, but as I pointed out in a speech, "Biochemical Research on Alcoholism—A Critique," which I delivered in 1975 at a Symposium on Alcoholism sponsored by the National Center for Toxicological Research in Little Rock, Arkansas (see Appendix II), most of those who have studied in this field make the tacit assumption that if we knew how *the human body* metabolizes alcohol we would understand alcoholism. This is fallacious. We need to know how different human bodies metabolize alcohol in unique ways and with unique results. The speech referred to above has been printed in its entirety in Appendix II because it is comprehensive and, with its substantial bibliography, will give the reader some idea of the character and extent of investigations currently under way in the field of alcoholism. The extent of this investigation is impressive, but I fear much of it is pointless, because the investigators are often so oblivious to inborn biochemical individuality.

One of our first experimental studies (1949), which demonstrated beyond question the need for paying attention to individuals, involved giving a series of twenty rats, in separate cages, a choice between water and ten-percent alcohol as a beverage. We switched the positions of the drinking bottles often and the individual animals had to sniff and choose. We observed four different types of responses. Some animals drank very little alcohol at any time; some drank only a little at first but later drank much larger amounts; some drank heavily at the first and continued to do so; some drank for a few days, abstained for a few days, and then returned to drink somewhat periodically.

Some "tunnel vision" investigators dismissed these findings as lacking pertinence, since rats do not become "alcoholics" and do not even become drunk. They missed the clear point that individual rats react in a most distinctive fashion to beverage alcohol, and that some have a biological urge to drink, while others do not.

No one should expect, we thought, a precise parallel between rats and humans, so we continued our explorations to find out (1) why the individual animals differed from each other so much, and (2) why some chose to drink while others did not.

Our explorations, lasting for several years and involving many investigators and large numbers of rats, were productive. We found the answers to both questions: (1) The individual rats differed from each other because of *inherited* differences in their body metabolism. We found, for example, that the urinary excretion patterns of individual rats differed *markedly* from each other even though the rats looked alike and were from the same inbred strain. (2) We traced the reason why some rats consumed alcohol by choice and others did not to the quality of the nutrition of the individual animals. When an animal abstained from alcohol, he was receiving a diet satisfactorily complete for him as an individual. If an animal tended to drink alcohol freely, his diet was deficient in some respect.

We performed many hundreds of experiments in our laboratories, and we established beyond any question the close relationship between diet and the biological urge to drink alcohol.

In some experiments we deliberately left out a particular vitamin from the diet of a rat. This would cause him to drink at high levels, but when we put the missing vitamin back into his diet his alcohol consumption dropped dramatically, often overnight, from a high value to a very low one.

We conducted experiments of this type (taking a

vitamin out of and later putting it back into the diet) with vitamin A, thiamin, riboflavin, pantothenic acid, and vitamin B_6. A deficiency of any one of these vitamins caused increased alcohol consumption. When we returned the vitamin to the diet, the alcohol consumption always fell markedly.

By 1951 we had accumulated a large amount of data, which we published in a 205-page bulletin, "Individual Metabolic Patterns and Human Disease" (University of Texas Publication No. 5109, May, 1951). This bulletin contained a series of twenty-two articles and represented the work of fifteen investigators.

We found that every individual animal and every individual human being has a highly distinctive "metabolic pattern" as judged by numerous criteria. At that time, when many tools now available had not yet been developed, we studied primarily three areas in human beings: taste threshold, composition of salivas, and urinary excretions.

Each person we tested had a highly distinctive set of taste sensitivities to a series of chemicals; each person had a highly distinctive saliva; and each person had a highly distinctive urine composition. The differences involved were not of a few percent; often one person's value for a particular item was several times as great as the corresponding value of another person.

We studied a group of twelve individuals in these three ways, and the results are recorded in the following graphs. Each "star" diagram represents a particular individual who was supposedly "normal." Each line extending from the center represents quantitatively (by its length) a taste sensitivity, the amount of a saliva constituent, or the amount of a urinary constituent, as detailed in the caption below the diagrams.

FIGURE 1

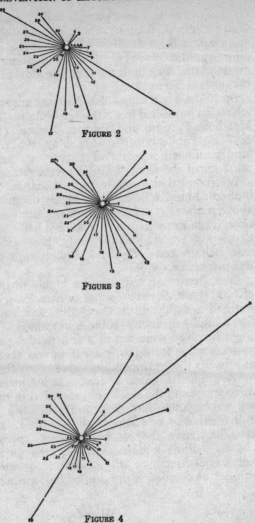

FIGURE 2

FIGURE 3

FIGURE 4

FIGS. 1–13. Taste Sensitivity: 1. Creatinine, 2. Sucrose, 3. KCl, 4. NaCl, 5. HCl. Salivary Constituents: 6. Uric acid, 7. Glucose, 8. Leucine, 9. Valine, 10. Citrulline, 11. Alanine, 12. Lysine, 13. Taurine, 14. Glycine, 15. Serine, 16. Glutamic acid, 17. Aspartic acid.

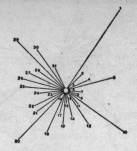

FIGURE 5

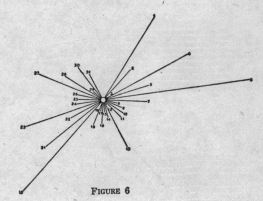

FIGURE 6

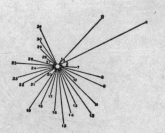

FIGURE 7

(contd.) Urinary Constituents: 18. Citrate, 19. Base Rf.28, 20. Acid Rf.32, 21. Gonadotropin, 22. pH, 23. Pigment/creatinine, 24. Chloride/creatinine, 25. Hippuric acid/creatinine, 26. Creatinine, 27. Taurine, 28. Glycine, 29. Serine, 30. Citrulline, 31. Alanine.

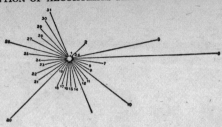

FIGURE 8

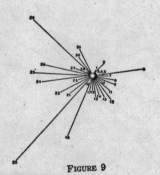

FIGURE 9

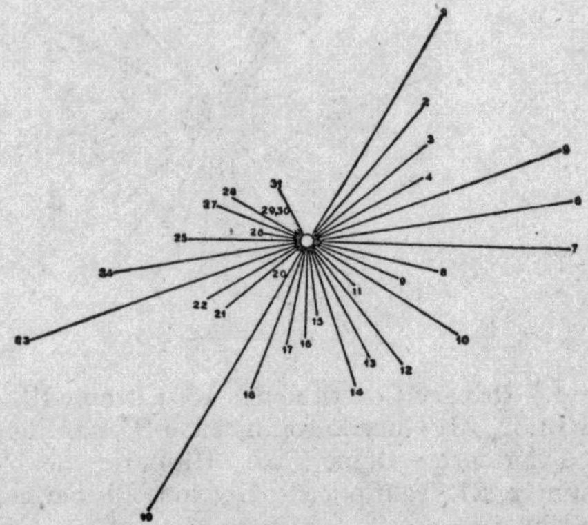

FIGURE 10

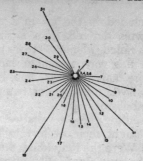

FIGURE 11

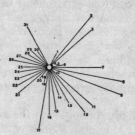

FIGURE 12

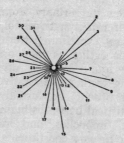

FIGURE 13

We included in the group a pair of monozygous twins (twins derived from a single egg, often erroneously called *"identical"* twins). Their patterns, depicted in this way, resemble each other (#12 and #13) more than any other two, but still they are not identical. Even monozygous twins do not have identical metabolisms.

In presenting these results we were not unmindful of what might seem at first to be an embarrassing question: Were the individuals we were testing eating exactly the same food? The answer is no, they were eating in their accustomed manner. Practically, this is the only regimen that one can follow in such an experiment.

We tried to conduct experiments in which we could determine the urinary excretion patterns of a few individuals eating the same food. We found, somewhat to our surprise, that it is virtually impossible to get a series of individuals to eat precisely the same food. However, even when they ate approximately the same things, their urinary excretion patterns remained distinctive.

No two individual people eat the same (nor do any two individual animals). The way they eat is an expression of their individuality. The diagrams we present above reflect differences in eating behavior as well as differences in internal metabolism.

In experiments in which we made extensive comparisons between the urinary excretion patterns of "retarded" children in a state school, we were able to show that urinary excretion patterns (data obtained from individuals eating as they ordinarily eat) are significant. We found that by urinary examination alone (involving testing quantitatively for a number of unusual constituents not usually tested for) we could, on a statistical basis, distinguish between "normals," "morons," "imbeciles," and "idiots." Some of the tests for specific urinary constituents showed extremely high degrees of statistical significance.

An extremely interesting observation came to light when we studied, for comparative purposes, the urinary excretion patterns of a group of "normal" school children. One of my coworkers noted that one individual in the group of "normals" seemed to exhibit unusual peculiarities in the urinary excretion pattern reminiscent of those obtained from "retarded" children. Up to that time we had paid no attention to the "I.Q.'s" of the individual normal children. We had looked at them merely as a group. Later we were allowed to study the confidential I.Q. scores of all the children in the group. The one individual which my coworker had spotted by urinary examination to be reminiscent of "retarded" children had the lowest I.Q. of anyone in the group. In addition, her teachers considered her a problem child, since she, though coming from an affluent home, had been caught stealing from her classmates.

These studies impressed me very much. However, the scientific world paid little attention to them. We published these findings in the bulletin cited above and we distributed copies to numerous individuals and to the leading libraries in the country.

At the time this work was done it was not fashionable to study individual people. No journals existed for publishing the results of these studies. Furthermore, economic necessity forced my students who had been studying individuality to change their research activities to some other field after they left the university. Research is difficult when a strong tide of scientific opinion is running in opposition. The situation has not changed materially in the twenty-five years since we published this collection of papers on individual metabolic patterns. It is not surprising, then, that the why of alcoholic vulnerability remains in a fog.

While we were studying human individuality we also continued our earlier animal experiments. Because nutrition greatly influences the consumption of alcohol by rats and mice we suspected that human nutrition would greatly influence human consumption of alcohol. Since individuality greatly influences nutrition, two individuals may eat approximately the same food and their nourishment may still be at different levels of excellence. Theoretically, and probably in actual life as well, one individual may receive poor nourishment from a diet that is excellent for another. As I have noted before, Lucretius said centuries ago, "What is one man's meat may be another's poison."

We came to the tentative conclusion that individuals who are extremely vulnerable to alcohol have unusual nutritional needs, and food that is satisfactory to many others may not adequately nourish them. When these vulnerable individuals consume alcohol, they greatly aggravate the situation. If the vulnerable individual consumes alcohol heavily and for a prolonged period, he or she poisons body metabolism and causes the derangement of all regulatory mechanisms.

Following up this idea, we furnished nutritional supplements to alcoholics and some whom the disease threatened, in the hope that the supplements would benefit them. The results for some were dramatic and consistent; for others the benefits were only slight. We interpreted the failures to mean that the supplement was not quite the right one for them individually. We had had similar results with experimental animals. The same supplement did not act uniformly for individual rats or for rats from different colonies.

The results were so promising that in 1951 I published a book, *Nutrition and Alcoholism* (University of Oklahoma Press), which set forth our ideas and presented our findings.

In connection with this book I encountered the same problem of misinterpretation that later plagued the writers of the "Rand" report, *Alcoholism and Treatment* (1976). In a case I have also cited earlier in this book, an alcoholic whom a physician treated with nutritional supplements that I recommended derived dramatic benefit, as long as he took the supplement. When I saw him about a year after he first took the cure he told me he was still taking the supplement and had fully recovered. He also told me that he still occasionally drank socially but had no further craving for alcohol. I recorded this experience in *Nutrition and Alcoholism*.

Unfortunately, the description of this case was interpreted to mean that I recommended that recovered alcoholics try to drink socially. This was not my recommendation. However, since this feature of my book offended Alcoholics Anonymous and other influential people in the field of alcoholism, I purchased and destroyed the remaining copies of the book and withdrew it from circulation. At the same time I wrote a new book, *Alcoholism: The Nutritional Approach,* and dedicated it to Alcoholics Anonymous as a peace offering.

In the Rand report, Drs. Davis Armor, J. Michael Polich, and Harriet Stambul tell of cases in which alcoholics have become social drinkers. If the press plays up this point, as has been done in part by the critics of the Rand report, this *suggests* (regardless of explanations) that alcoholics may try to become social drinkers. This suggestion is actually a strong one because the public as a whole knows little about inborn individuality and it is commonplace to assume that what one person can do another can also do.

The risk involved when an alcoholic tries to become a social drinker is very high indeed and I *do not ever recommend taking this risk.* I know many recovered alcoholics who live happily without alcohol, and I believe most could do this if they were able to adjust their inner environments to a high level of excellence.

It appears that the writers of the Rand report made the common assumption, as a matter of course, that there will always be alcoholics and that they will all face the same dilemma. If people adopt the ideas I present in this book we can prevent alcoholism as a major problem, in which case the question becomes unimportant because then all people who drink can *remain* social drinkers if they want to and no one will need to reach the point where control is lost. If the general public, including high school and college students, were to get the kind of nutrition education set forth in my book, *The Wonderful World Within You* (Bantam Books), this would tremendously facilitate the prevention of alcoholism and hasten the day when no one will have to answer the question, "Should I, as an alcoholic, try to return to social drinking?"

I find myself unable to escape from the fundamental

idea that everyone has or can have substantial control over his or her life and therefore has a corresponding responsibility to captain his or her ship wisely. Alcohol will "get" no one unless he or she cooperates, either in ignorance or with wide-open eyes. People who have become alcoholics have done so because they have been ignorant about their internal environment and have joined with others in the common, often disastrous notion that it is perfectly all right and in no way reprehensible to drink without inhibitions, as much and as frequently as one's appetite and ability to pay dictate. The idea that there is something commendable and honorable about consuming large quantities of liquor, even something to brag about, is a thoroughly silly one. It would be just as silly for someone to brag about being able to sniff chloroform all day without becoming anesthetized. If we continue to hold on to such ideas, it is inevitable that we will pay the price of an ever increasing rate of alcoholism.

Shortly after the publication of my first book on the subject, *Nutrition and Alcoholism*, I assisted Dr. Fred Stare of Harvard in gaining support for an experiment he contemplated. Outpatient alcoholics were the subjects in this experiment. One group took nutritional supplements in the form of several vitamins, while another group took placebos (blanks) that resembled the supplements given the first group.

On the basis of what we know now, several factors made this an imperfect test of the nutritional hypothesis. (1) They used only certain vitamins (limited in number) and no minerals; they did not use glutamine, which subsequent investigations have shown to be highly promising for alcoholics. (2) They gave five kinds of capsules or tablets to the alcoholics for daily administration, and excellent circumstantial evidence indicated that the alcoholics did not consistently take what they were supposed to be taking. (3) The "treated" and the "placebo" groups did not maintain their identity during the experiment. (The experimenters evidently thought, on humane grounds, that they should shift some of the "placebo" group into the "treated" group in order to give them the benefit.)

In spite of these imperfections, each one of which militated *against* making the treatment appear successful, the results were promising, as is shown in the summary of the paper published in the *Journal of the American Medical Association* (May, 1954).

While the results of the treatment of alcoholism by means of dietary supplements were somewhat disappointing on a group basis, there is evidence that a number of patients were benefited. Of the 32 alcoholic patients who took part in the nutritional study for 13 months or more, 25 had vitamin medication and 7 continued with placebos. Of those taking vitamins, seven patients were abstinent, seven were controlled, two were improved, and nine exhibited no change, while, of those taking the placebos, one was abstinent, and six exhibited no change. The fact that the number of patients taking vitamins was larger than the number taking placebos was because many of the patients were in such extreme circumstances that placebo therapy was not justified.

There is evidence that not all the patients took the medication prescribed, and this factor inevitably operates to diminish the apparent effectiveness of the treatment. The results of this study do not suggest optimism with respect to widespread benefits to be derived from presently available vitamin medication; it does, however, indicate that some persons are benefited by vitamin therapy. The results are sufficiently favorable to warrant additional research on the effects of nutritional supplements in the treatment of alcoholism and on the studies of metabolism of alcohol.

That researchers have not followed up this promising experiment in the past twenty-five years is pathetic. They have even cited it as negative evidence. The principal reason for neglecting it is a general failure on the part of those medical investigators concerned with alcoholism to appreciate the facts of inborn individuality. Every alcoholic has his or her own unique metabolic problem. Because of this, if the researchers had given all the "treated" alcoholics a more complete assortment of promising nutrients, including minerals and glutamine, probably every one would have benefited greatly. This gross neglect of a very promising lead is the result of ignorance of metabolic individuality.

Over the course of several years in our laboratories we made a number of attempts to find out what peculiarities in the metabolisms of certain individuals make them vulnerable to alcoholism. One of the difficulties we encountered is metabolic variations between ethnic groups. We found, for example, certain characteristics to be significantly distinctive when we limited ourselves to Caucasians. However, as soon as we included other ethnic groups the tests failed to be dependable.

In our earlier work we depended to a considerable extent on urinary excretion patterns. Later we exhaustively studied amino acid patterns in the blood. Each individual has a distinctive pattern of amino acids in the blood, and we can now relatively easily determine these chromatographically. Some of the more recent work in this field was conducted by my coworkers and former students, Drs. Frank Siegel and Leon Pomeroy. It indicates that these innate distinctive patterns may be most useful. By using appropriately refined procedures, it should be possible to spot potential alcoholics before they have any trouble.

Before substantial progress can come in the field of alcoholism, however, more investigators must be sold on the idea that inborn individuality is a fact of life and plays a tremendously important role in alcoholism.

One of my former students, Dr. Charles Williams (Bill) Bode (Appendix III, p. 153, #13), carried out, in the College of Pharmacy at the University of Texas at Austin, a series of experiments that point unmistakably to the importance of individuality in the broad alcoholism problem. He administered, by injection, carefully adjusted doses of alcohol to one hundred mice—each mouse got the same dose on a body weight basis. The dosage was enough to put the mice to sleep, but they remained asleep for differing lengths of time —from twenty-five minutes to two hundred fifty minutes. The mice were inbred albinos. If the mice had been a heterogeneous group of vastly different ancestries, the spread would have presumably been much greater and some animals might have resisted sleep and others might have died.

Dr. Bode could have presented the results of this experiment in the form of a "normal distribution curve" and treated them statistically in a pedestrian manner, but he was not interested in this. He was concerned with the question, *Why* are some mice resistant to and others sensitive to alcohol depression? Is this due to inborn metabolic differences in the individual mice?

The first evidence supporting an affirmative answer to the last question was the fact that when he tested *the same* one hundred mice again at a later time, they behaved in accordance with the earlier experiment. The "short sleepers" in the first experiment were the short sleepers the second time around, and the long sleepers were the same individual mice in both experiments. Furthermore, Dr. Bode found that the more resistant mice had more coenzyme I in their brains than the susceptible mice.

Anyone capable of interpreting animal experiments would logically conclude from these experiments and other corroborating evidence that in all probability some inborn metabolic peculiarity in the makeup of potential alcoholics causes them to be susceptible to alcohol addiction.

In a different study another former student, Dr. Mary K. Roach (Appendix III, p. 147, #21), demonstrated that alcohol administration does fundamentally affect the metabolism in the brain by impairing its ability to use its prime fuel—glucose. Both of these studies emphasize the importance of the metabolic aspects of alcoholism.

Members of Alcoholics Anonymous, as laymen, have recognized for decades that there are some things in their makeup that they cannot correct, and that susceptibility to alcohol poisoning is one of them. This is a manifestation of inborn individuality. If medical scientists recognized the facts of inborn individuality and incorporated them into their thinking, a tremendous forward step would be taken in attacking the alcoholism problem.

Several years ago another of my former students, Dr. Eleanor Storrs, studied the anatomies and certain biochemical parameters of sixteen sets of quadruplet armadillos at birth (Appendix III, p. 81, #8). These studies, broadly interpreted in the light of previous experiments with inbred strains of rats, mice, and hamsters, lead inevitably to the conclusion that in the whole mammalian kingdom monozygous twins and quadruplets are *not* metabolically identical. Whatever the detailed mechanism of mammalian inheritance is, it results in the production of monozygous twins and quadruplets that *resemble* each other in their metabolic makeup but at the same time differ substantially and sometimes strikingly. Dr. Storrs found hormone levels and amino acid levels in the brain to differ manyfold in some cases.

Since inborn individuality extends even to *identical* twins, we must discard the numerous studies built upon the assumption that monozygous twins have identical inheritance.

I have cited other doctoral dissertations that I have supervised relating to inborn individuality in the bibliography at the end of this book. Due to the unfashionable nature of many of these studies and the unfavorable scientific climate of the times, traditional journals would not publish them.

I cannot emphasize too strongly that leaving inborn individuality out of the study of the problem deals the whole investigation of alcoholism a body blow, making progress impossible.

Many investigators, although supposedly directing their research toward alcoholism, are, in reality, directing it toward the "hypothetical man," whose metabolic pattern does not exist (see patternless Figure 1, p. 87).

Figures 2 through 13 represent real people; real people require study.

Psychiatrists and psychologists who hope to help alcoholics simply through psychoanalysis base their efforts on irrationality. The facts of inborn individuality make this an impossible hope. Real analysis of one's psyche would involve a complete grasp of the uniqueness of one's brain structure, neurology, sensory equipment, and endocrinology by the psychiatrist or psychologist who does the analyzing. Psychoanalysis of hypothetical, patternless man (Figure 1, p. 87) is, in relation to real people, a scientific joke.

21

Exclusion From Medical Thinking of the Concept of Quality Control of Nutritional Cellular Environments

Physicians and medical scientists have several different attitudes toward nutrition and its place in the scheme of things and in the promotion of health.

Some say, "Of course we are interested in vitamins and nutrition. We accept that vitamin B_1 will cure beriberi, vitamin C will cure scurvy, niacinamide will cure pellagra, vitamin B_{12} will cure pernicious anemia, vitamin D may cure rickets. When someone comes up with a vitamin that will cure heart disease or any disease that is prevalent today, we will surely use it."

Individual physicians with this attitude would probably say that nutrition has little or nothing to do with mental retardation, heart disease (except when you eat cholesterol or grow fat), mental disease, alcoholism, or cancer. Those who have this complacent attitude do not understand how nutrients function physiologically. They have a completely uninformed view of the nutritional process.

Some physicians and medical scientists say, "Nutrition is important, but all one has to do is to eat well-balanced meals to get anything needed." This statement indicates a serious lack of appreciation of the approximately forty different nutrient chemicals we need to obtain from our environment and how, in practical circumstances, these work together to yield every degree of metabolic efficiency from vigorous health to serious generalized cytopathy in which all cells in the body suffer.

The majority of physicians and medical scientists have an attitude different from both of these. They neither affirm nor deny the importance of nutrition. They say *nothing*. Although attitudes are changing, many physicians avoid discussing the subject of nutrition with their patients.

Why is it that physicians have so little to say about nutrition? Why do medical scientists seldom bring nutrition into their conversation? "Lack of education" is an answer, but it leads to the question, "*Why* has there been lack of education?"

One of the prime reasons why medical scientists are unenthusiastic about nutritional education is that untutored enthusiasts (quacks and food faddists) have given nutrition a bad name. Some of the worst books on nutrition have been written by faddist physicians. Understandably, their colleagues have been loath to join hands with incompetents. Physicians in general have a legitimate and laudable desire to be respectable. Hence, they keep quiet.

Physicians often base their resistance to vitamins and nutrition on the legitimate fear that people will practice self-medication and thus fail to get expert help.

It is possible that physicians and medical scientists hesitate to get into the complex subject of nutrition partly because of the intuitive feeling that it will lead them into the morass of cell metabolism. Individuality in nutrition would come into play and this is a sticky subject.

My associate, Dr. Man-Li Yew, searched the literature for information about how amino acid and other nutrient needs vary from individual to individual and came up with the following tabulation:

RANGES OF DAILY HUMAN NEEDS
FOR CERTAIN NUTRIENTS*

Nutrient	Range	No. Subjects	Reference
Tryptophan	82–250 mg (3-fold)	50	3,4
Valine	375–800 mg (2.1-fold)	48	3,5
Phenylalanine	420–1,100 mg (2.6-fold)	38	3,6
Leucine	170–1,100 mg (6.4-fold)	31	3,7
Lysine	400–2,800 mg (7-fold)	55	3,8,9
Isoleucine	250–700 mg (2.8-fold)	24	3,10
Methionine	800–3,000 mg (3.7-fold)	29	3,9
Threonine	103–500 mg (4.8-fold)	50	3,11
Calcium	222–1,018 mg (4.6-fold)	19	12
Thiamin	0.4–1.59 mg (3.9-fold)	15	13

In addition to the items listed, there are two vitamins for which the individual needs are uncertain and vary enormously, according to the best available evidence—vitamin A and vitamin C.*

The conservative, authoritative *Heinz Handbook of Nutrition* states plainly and unequivocally that the typical person probably has some nutritional needs that are *far from average.* Yet the medical scientists on the Food and Nutrition Board in Washington when establishing their Recommended Daily Allowances often neglect the established facts of individuality and assume that individual needs usually vary perhaps 25, 50, or possibly 100 percent rather than *several fold* as is actually the case. This can make a great difference in the strategy of individual nutritional management. Medical scientists seem to find it difficult to

*The reference numbers in the table refer to the bibliography of the article entitled "A Renaissance of Nutritional Science Is Imminent," by Roger J. Williams, James D. Heffley, Man-Li Yew, and Charles W. Bode, *Perspectives in Biology and Medicine*, Vol. 17, No. 1, Autumn 1973. In this article there are other references and a discussion of variation in nutritional needs.

squarely face the facts of nutritional individuality.

There are five sets of facts about nutrition that many physicians and medical scientists do not fully recognize. Lack of appreciation of these facts easily leads to the assumption that nutrition has nothing to do with alcoholism. Once they have grasped the truth and significance of these sets of facts, no question will remain about the probable connection between alcoholism and nutrition.

These sets of facts are:

1. We must obtain the approximately forty known nutrient chemicals from our environment in the same sense that we obtain oxygen and water. They are just as essential to life. We need all these nutrient chemicals to build the metabolic machinery of life. We have almost no storage capacity for oxygen, hence we need it minute by minute. For water and many of the nutrient chemicals we have varying storage capacities. As a result we do not need to take in the nutrients every minute as we do oxygen. Some of the nutrients can be absent from our diet for days or even weeks, but eventually we must provide all of them, since we use each of them *every second of our lives*.

2. The nutrients are so numerous and the building of metabolic machinery so complex that under ordinary conditions of living the nutrients are never available to us in exactly the right proportions. Like other parts of our environment—the air we breathe, the water we drink, the weather we encounter, the fellow men we deal with—our nutritional environments *are always subject to improvement*.

3. Cellular nutrition and well-being are crucial. We consume food to keep all the cells in our bodies and in our brains well nourished and in good working order. Since we can nourish these cells at many different levels, they can be healthy or unhealthy at many different levels. Because of the way some people eat, their cellular nutrition may be far from ideal all the time. Cellular nutrition and well-being are always subject to improvement. When we improve our cellu-

lar environments, we improve our health. The patterns of our circulatory systems are so distinctive that we cannot take for granted that we are nourishing all the cells, organs, and tissues of our bodies equally well. Local impairments are probably often due to local circulatory problems. Total health comes only as a result of total nourishment. Physical exercise is an important factor in attaining the benefits of complete nourishment.

4. Individuality in nutrition is an ever present factor in everyone's life. The typical person has some needs that are far from average. Atypical persons are even farther from the average. Real people are often atypical in diverse ways. These are the people whom disease is likely to attack. A tremendous amount of biological evidence makes it most reasonable to postulate that alcoholics have distinctive metabolisms that make them vulnerable to the kind of alcohol poisoning that results in seriously deranged appetite mechanisms. For these individuals the traditional "Recommended Daily Allowances," which had their origin decades ago before the facts of biochemical individuality became known, are not applicable. These "allowances" have been set primarily for those who have few eccentricities.

It is not accidental that individual people do not share the same tastes and the same eating behavior. It appears certain that there is, on the part of distinctive individuals, an attempt to compensate for their differing nutritional needs. We know for a fact that the inborn individuality of experimental animals includes highly distinctive tendencies to choose their food very differently.

"Body wisdom," which helps individuals get the nutrients they need, is not always perfect. In alcoholics —the compulsive drinkers—"body wisdom" has changed to "body foolishness."

5. Nutrients in physiology always cooperate *constructively*. Metabolic machinery contains many working parts and every nutrient has its part to play in the process of metabolism. When vitamin B$_1$ "cures beri-

beri," for example, it does so by contributing one link to a weakened metabolic chain. In persons who are victims of beriberi, the food they consume contains all the other nutrient chemicals in amounts sufficient to maintain life except for a sorely needed quantity of vitamin B_1. When we furnish vitamin B_1, normal metabolism can proceed in a healthy manner. For a beriberi patient to recover his or her health completely, it is absolutely essential that he or she receive good food containing adequate amounts of *all* the essential nutrient chemicals. The whole metabolic team works together to bring back health.

Nutrients act entirely differently from drugs or medicines, which, as we indicated earlier, do not act constructively but confer their benefits by altering the course of metabolism in a way that seems temporarily advantageous. Drugs and medicines are no good for a steady diet. Competent doctors recognize this and seek to use drugs only temporarily. Nutrients—the minerals, amino acids, and vitamins—in contrast to drugs, are mandatory ingredients of a steady, lifetime diet. We need them all as a team to promote life and health.

With these five basic points in mind, the way is clear for medical scientists. They can move toward prevention intelligently and can also develop successful and adequate treatments for those who have slipped into alcoholism. Alcoholism can cease to be a disaster area in medicine. It can become an area where productive results are obtainable and medical science can be proud because of its capabilities. We cannot do this without intelligent attention to nutritional environments.

22

The Universal Role of Cellular Environments in Making Life and Health Possible

The theme of this book centers on the idea that building a strong internal cellular environment will promote internal health and prevent alcoholism. The need for fully adequate cellular environments, which has many applications aside from alcoholism, is by no means a fly-by-night idea. I began to get acquainted with it in 1918. It is not a hypothetical, untried, or speculative idea but has matured and proved itself over several decades. A tremendous wealth of evidence supports it. The idea applies to the entire world of biology.

In 1918 I embarked as a graduate student at the University of Chicago on my doctorate training; a fellowship from the Fleischmann Company supported me. The problem set before me was essentially to study how to produce a suitable environment for yeast cells. It is evident that cellular environments have been in my mind for a long period of time. Following up on this initial work, I discovered, about ten years later, an environmental substance, pantothenic acid. Yeast cells require it; not only is this so, but, as we now know, every cell in our body requires it. About fifteen years later we discovered and concentrated for the first time another vitamin, folic acid; at this time we were seeking a way to improve the environment of the cells of certain lactic acid bacteria. All the cells of our body also use this vitamin, folic acid. Cellular environments were still central to my interest.

The cellular environments of single-celled organisms like yeast cells or bacterial cells absolutely dominate their existence and welfare. Whether these cells live or die, or are healthy or unhealthy, depends entirely on the environments surrounding them.

Likewise, in multicellular organisms there is always an internal environment that bathes the many cells, and the character of this internal environment determines the life, death, and health of individual cells and of the whole organism.

Our food plants, like corn or wheat, have their internal environments (plant sap); the quality of the environments surounding these cells determines the health of the cells that make up these plants. The size of the crop (the bushels per acre) depends entirely on the quality of the internal environments of the crop plants. A field of corn, for example, can produce as little as five bushels per acre (nubbins), or it can produce one hundred and fifty bushels of corn per acre in full ears.

The quality of these internal environments differs enormously in practical agriculture. Water is an important factor, and so is the fertility of the soil. Fertile soil contains all the minerals and trace elements—zinc, manganese, copper, iron, molybdenum, etc.—we need in our internal environments. These are essential to the life and productivity of the plants.

When we study laboratory animals to determine the best conditions for their growth, reproduction, and health, we can alter their internal environments with most profound results. We can maintain their internal environments at different levels—poor, mediocre, good, or excellent—with the result that the quality of their lives is correspondingly poor, mediocre, good, or excellent.

These findings with respect to laboratory animals also apply to pets, farm animals, and poultry. Producers have revolutionized the raising of chickens for meat in recent decades by realizing that if they give baby chicks the wherewithal to build a really excellent internal environment, they grow, develop, and produce good meat at an extremely rapid rate. If the poultry raisers were to furnish them environmental stuff of low quality the chickens would dwindle and die.

Those who raise trout, salmon, or catfish in hatcheries have likewise revolutionized their operations by recognizing that they need to supply the tiny newly-hatched fish with suitable amounts of all the environmental elements they need. When this is done, growth takes place with unheard-of speed.

A tremendous biochemical unity exists in all of nature. Wherever we look we see the marvelous importance of cellular environments. Take bees, for example. We may note that when the queen bee lays thousands of fertile eggs they yield larvae, the development of which depends on the cellular environments resulting from the food they receive. If we furnish the larvae routine food, they develop into short-lived, sterile "worker bees." If they get special food ("royal jelly"), the larvae develop into much larger, fertile "queens" which may live twenty to thirty times as long. The difference between a "worker bee" and a "queen" reflects the contrast between the cellular environments the larvae receive during development.

There is tremendous unity in nature in another way. The cellular environments that are favorable to the life of entirely different organisms show strong resemblances. The very same nutrient chemicals that enter into the metabolic machinery of yeasts, bacteria, insects, fish, oysters, corn, wheat, cotton, fowls, rats, snakes, pigs, and cattle also enter into the makeup of human metabolic processes.

Surely, if cellular environments are of the utmost importance for all other forms of life, they must also be crucially important for human life and health. The validity of the basic idea we present in this book rests upon this broad premise, which no informed person can question.

There are many other applications of this broad-gauged principle. Upgrading one's internal environment produces vast benefits aside from preventing trouble with alcohol.

In a book, *Nutrition Against Disease,* I have proposed, discussed, and defended the proposition that we can prevent and treat many prevalent diseases when medical scientists "get on the ball" and utilize the vast possibilities of adjusting internal environments by careful scrutiny of what nutrient chemicals enter our bodies.

If the inner environment of a pregnant woman is of high quality, the chances are excellent that she will give birth to a baby free from major and minor defects of body and brain. Extensive experience with experimental animals has led us to this conclusion. They give birth to healthy young when their internal environments are excellent, but often give birth to defective young if the internal environments are mediocre in quality. When the internal environments of pregnant female animals are deliberately made defective, they produce deformed offspring.

By maintaining high quality inner environments, middle-aged men could probably prevent heart attacks. This is not a simple problem and does not have a simple answer like "Avoid cholesterol in the diet." This answer appears an obvious one but is probably a wrong one. Many *excellent* foods contain cholesterol, which is, incidentally, a necessary constituent of our bodies; many of our body cells produce it.

If we provide young children (and pregnant women) with excellent internal environments, children and young people will have good, sound teeth. Dental troubles will largely vanish.

When people reach middle age, they often become arthritic and their joints fail to function well. There must be something wrong with their internal environments. Deficiencies or imbalances must exist. This too is not a simple problem. Certainly arthritis does not arise from a bodily deficiency of aspirin. Aspirin is foreign to the body and probably never existed on earth before chemists made it in the laboratory. Yet, more often than not, doctors prescribe aspirin in relatively large doses and for relatively long periods of time for patients suffering from arthritis.

Mental illness is a terrible scourge and does not arise because of a bodily deficiency of tranquilizers or other drugs. Something must be wrong with the inner environment surrounding the brain cells.

The prevention of all these troubles is not something that we can easily demonstrate at present. That will require much patient research and exploration. Medical scientists by the thousands need to participate.

If internal environments are not to blame for these troubles, we have no place to turn. With all the vast array of environmental factors to explore, it is nonsensical to neglect all of them and suppose that heredity is to blame. Of course, we are by inheritance different from one another, but if each individual obtains an environment suitable for him or her as an individual, then each individual can attain healthy growth, development, and maintenance.

Internal environments offer a vast unexplored territory for human betterment. The neglect of these environments by medical scientists, even if we look at it in a charitable light, constitutes one of the dark pages in medical history.

Better days are ahead. Physicians and medical scientists are now recognizing more and more that the internal environment that each of us carries with him all the time is a vital factor in all health problems.

Appendix I

Nutritional Supplements

I extensively discussed the role of nutritional supplements in general in chapter 9 of my *Physician's Handbook of Nutritional Science* (1975). The supplements I mention in *this* book on alcoholism prevention are those that I recommend to prevent this particular disease.

The first supplement that I devised for alcoholism was given to the public and was marketed by Eli Lilly and Company under the name of "Tycopan." This supplement contained only vitamins, because at the time (1951) I did not fully appreciate the need for the complete nutritional team to protect against alcoholism. Tycopan is still available but, because of its substantial content of folic acid, is obtainable only by prescription.

About ten years later I formulated supplements containing both vitamins and minerals for general use as well as for alcoholism prevention. These were given to the public and sold under different names by different firms—"Nutricol" and "Nutricol Forte" by Vitamin Quota of New York and Los Angeles; "Formula P 127" by Walgreen Drugstores; and "G-154 Nutrins" by General Nutrition Corporation stores.

As nutritional science has progressed (slowly) modifications have been made in the recommended supplements. The "Formulation for Nutritional Insurance," as set forth in my *Physician's Handbook of Nutritional Science,* has a composition similar in most respects to that given in the first of the two following tables:

CURRENTLY SUGGESTED FORMULATION FOR NUTRITIONAL INSURANCE*†

Vitamin components		Mineral components	
Vitamin A	7,500 units	Calcium	250 mg
Vitamin D	400 units	Phosphate	750 mg
Vitamin E	40 units		(equivalent
Vitamin K			to 250 mg
(Menedione)	2 mg		phosphorus)
Ascorbic Acid	250 mg	Magnesium	200 mg
Thiamin	2 mg	Iron	15 mg
Riboflavin	2 mg	Zinc	15 mg
Vitamin B_6	3 mg	Copper**	1 mg
Vitamin B_{12}	9 mcg	Iodine	0.15 mg
Niacinamide	20 mg	Manganese	5 mg
Pantothenic Acid	15 mg	Molybdenum	0.1 mg
Biotin	0.3 mg	Chromium	1 mg
Folic Acid	0.4 mg	Selenium	0.05 mg
Choline	250 mg	Cobalt	0.1 mg
Inositol	250 mg		
P-aminobenzoic			
Acid	30 mg		
Rutin	200 mg		

*This is my designation, not a trade name, and suppliers can designate it as they wish. The formula has been given to the public and, as stated before, I have no financial interest in it. If any of the items are excluded by FDA regulations, manufacturers will, of course, have to comply. Also, medical supervision is advised for all who choose to take substantial doses of these supplements, even if a prescription is not required.

†These suggested vitamin and mineral supplements, designed primarily for adults, can be used without change for teenagers as well. For younger children the amounts in each case can be diminished under medical supervision to one-third of the suggested amounts for adults. For young children who consume mostly milk, the iron supplement for adults would probably not be too high. Knowledge regarding the needs at different ages is limited, so that hair-splitting discriminations cannot safely be made.

**Some students of supplementation think that individuals (especially when they have copper plumbing) tend to get *too much* copper. Suppliers, if the trade demands it, may wish to furnish this supplement without any copper.

CURRENTLY SUGGESTED *FORTIFIED* FORMULATION
FOR NUTRITIONAL INSURANCE*

Vitamin components		Mineral components	
Vitamin A	15,000 units	Calcium	250 mg
Vitamin D	400 units	Phosphate	750 mg
Vitamin E	400 units		(equivalent
Vitamin K			to 250 mg
(Menedione)	2 mg		phosphorus)
Ascorbic Acid	2,500 mg	Magnesium	200 mg
Thiamin	20 mg	Iron	30 mg
Riboflavin	20 mg	Zinc	30 mg
Vitamin B_6	30 mg	Copper**	2 mg
Vitamin B_{12}	90 mcg	Iodine	0.3 mg
Niacinamide	200 mg	Manganese	10 mg
Pantothenic Acid	150 mg	Molybdenum	0.2 mg
Biotin	3 mg	Chromium	2 mg
Folic Acid†	4 mg	Selenium	0.10 mg
Choline	500 mg	Cobalt	0.2 mg
Inositol	500 mg		
P-aminobenzoic			
Acid	30 mg		
Rutin	200 mg		

*This is my designation, not a trade name, and suppliers can designate it as they wish. The formula has been given to the public and, as stated before, I have no financial interest in it. If any of the items are excluded by FDA regulations, manufacturers will, of course, have to comply. Also, medical supervision is advised for all who choose to take substantial doses of these supplements, even if a prescription is not required.

†This amount of folic acid can be obtained with a doctor's prescription.

**Some students of supplementation think that individuals (especially when they have copper plumbing) tend to get *too much* copper. Suppliers, if the trade demands it, may wish to furnish this supplement without any copper.

When the "Formulation for Nutritional Insurance" was first set forth in my *Physician's Handbook of Nutritional Science* (1975), Bronson Pharmaceuticals (4526 Rinetti Lane, La Canada, California 91011), was the first to offer it for sale. Since the formulation was given to the public, any firm is free to market it. Besides Bronson Pharmaceuticals, the numerous General Nutrition Corporation Centers (General Offices, 418 Wood Street, Pittsburgh, Pa. 15222) and ICN Pharmaceuticals, Inc. (222 N. Vincent Ave., Covina, California 91722), have the same or similar supplements under their own trade names.

The currently suggested "*Fortified* Formulation for Nutritional Insurance" is available from the same sources as above and there is nothing to prevent other firms from following suit.

L-Glutamine is available from Erex Health Products (P.O. Box 278, Barnhart, Missouri 63012), Bronson Pharmaceuticals, the General Nutrition Corporation Centers, and others.

Appendix II

BIOCHEMICAL RESEARCH
ON ALCOHOLISM—A CRITIQUE
Roger J. Williams

(*Presented at the Symposium on Alcoholism sponsored by the National Center for Toxicological Research, September 5, 1975, in Little Rock, Arkansas.*)

A six-page representative bibliography of books, reviews, and a few journal articles covering the biochemical investigations related to alcoholism carried out during the past decade has been compiled by me with the help of associates, and has been placed in your hands.

I heard very recently of a type of symposium very different from this one. It involved undertakers. The topic under discussion was "How to appear sad at a $10,000 funeral."

My problem is just the opposite—"How to appear happy when a contemplation of this bibliography is depressing to me."

My feelings on them are greatly mitigated by the realization that in the National Center for Toxicological Research under the able leadership of Dr. Cranmer there will be no strong urge to follow beaten paths. In other words, the future of research on alcoholism cannot be predicted on the basis of past performances.

I will attempt to set forth briefly in a constructive way the reasons which impel me to be unenthusiastic about this record of biochemical research in this area.

My first contact with the problem of alcoholism

occurred when I published, nearly thirty years ago, in the *Quarterly Journal* a twenty-page article entitled "The Etiology of Alcoholism: A Working Hypothesis Involving the Interplay of Hereditary and Environmental Factors."[1]

A. J. Carlson of the University of Chicago paid this article a high compliment. He said it was the best thing ever written on the subject.

As perhaps the leading physiologist of his time and chairman of a national committee on alcoholism, he agreed with my tacit presumption that alcoholism is a physiological disease. Alcohol is a physiological agent and its use or abuse causes many physiological manifestations. This does not mean, however, that alcoholism is *exclusively* a physiological disease. It is also a psychological disease.

People are not built in compartments: physiological, biochemical, psychological, social. They are unified so that a disease as deep-seated as alcoholism affects every facet of one's existence and may have many diverse causes.

The fact that we have made so little progress in elucidating the etiology of alcoholism is due, in my opinion, to two fundamental deficiencies on the part of medical scientists and others who might explore in the area of this disease.

First, the general scientific public is practically totally unaware of the extent of the variations in anatomy, physiology, biochemistry, and psychology which exist in a population of "normal" newborn infants or in a population of "normal" adults.[2]

These detailed variations, when they can be measured numerically, are often five- or ten-fold and encompass the heart and circulatory system, the respiratory system, the digestive system, the muscular system, the endocrine system, the nervous system, the brain, and all the sense organs.

The fact of these variations, most conclusively evident in the area of anatomy, leads inevitably to the observation that every newborn infant possesses a distinctive individual pattern of his or her own. This pattern of interesting elements has a profound influence on the development and the activities of each of us. Each of us is distinctive, with a unique set of discordancies.

As I read books and reviews which purport to deal with biochemical research on alcoholism I see in them the underlying assumption that if we know all that alcohol does to man (how it affects every tissue and organ) and all that man does to alcohol (complete information as to how man metabolizes alcohol), the problem of alcoholism would be solved. About ninety percent of the research related to alcoholism seems to be based on this assumption.

This assumption is totally erroneous. Man (the average man if you will) does not become an alcoholic, even in our affluent and liquor-consuming culture. Only the exceptional man or woman becomes alcoholic; the unexceptional ones escape.

The facts of individuality, with which so many are unacquainted, are tremendously real factors in our lives. If we were not individually distinctive we would all have the same tastes, the same likes, dislikes, and inclinations. If this were so, we would all willingly go to the same schools, read the same books and newspapers, go to the same church, enjoy the same sports and recreation, go to bed and arise at the same times. Regimentation along the lines of our uniform desires would be perfectly acceptable and the love of liberty would be nonexistent.

If, as many assume, our individuality involves only trifling things: fingerprints, texture of hair, color of eyes, color and texture of skin, etc., then our love of liberty would be very limited and trifling. The fact that each of us has deep-seated distinctiveness in our entire individual makeup is reflected in the fact that our love of liberty is profound, inescapable, and worth fighting and dying for.

Alcoholism is not a problem of "man." It is a problem of real people, who are always distinctive individuals. Some of these individuals are peculiarly vulnerable. Until we study real people enough to find out the roots of individuality in alcoholism-proneness, we will not be able to fathom the question of the etiology of alcoholism.

There has been a strong tendency in the past to skirt around the central problem of alcoholism and to devote attention to ancillary problems. This, it seems to me, is characteristic of a large part of what normally, in the public eye, is devoted to alcoholism.

It is easier to try to answer such questions as: "What happens to alcohol in the body?" "What organs and tissues are affected by alcohol?" and "What diseases accompany alcoholism?" than it is to tackle the more complicated problem "Why do certain individuals become alcoholics while others are resistant?"

The time-honored publication, the *Quarterly Journal of Studies on Alcohol,* by its name encourages a scattering of effort and fails to promote a direct confrontation with the central problem of alcoholism. The current symposium we are attending is not designated as being concerned with alcoholism. Its title is "Alcohol—Problems and Research."

There are undeniably two prime factors which are involved in alcoholism: (1) alcohol itself and (2) the real people who are affected by it. In my judgment far too much attention has been paid to the study of alcohol and far too little to the study of real people. How would it be to have a journal devoted not to studies of alcohol, but rather to studies of real people? How about a symposium entitled "Real People—Problems and Research"?

Alcoholism is inaccurately designated as an "alcohol problem." More accurately it is a "people problem" involving alcohol.

The statement that real people always have marked individuality is based on a tremendous mass of evidence. One of the most conclusive studies bearing on this point was carried out in 1926 by Wade Brown and associates at the Rockefeller Institute. They dissected the bodies of 645 male rabbits and weighed their organs. The average and median differences in the organ weights of these rabbits were about ten-fold! Anyone who is biologically oriented will recognize that if such variation exists for male rabbits, a similar diversity must exist for male and female mammals of many sorts: squirrels, cats, dogs, monkeys, and human beings.[3]

RANGE IN RELATIVE
ORGAN WEIGHTS OF 645 RABBITS*

(Grams per kilo of net body weight)

Organ	Minimum	Maximum	Ratio of Max./Min.
Gastrointestinal mass	70.4	452.0	6
Heart	1.95	4.42	2.3
Liver	23.2	117.0	5
Kidneys	3.45	17.28	5
Spleen	0.035	2.93	80
Thymus	0.248	3.315	13
Testicles	0.47	4.93	10
Brain	3.33	8.16	2.5
Thyroid	0.048	1.23	25
Parathyroid	0.001	0.022	22
Hypophysis	0.007	0.035	5
Suprarenals	0.080	0.572	7
Pineal	0.002	0.025	12
Popliteal lymph nodes	0.05	0.382	8
Axillary lymph nodes	0.019	0.24	13
Deep cervical lymph nodes	0.02	0.295	15
Mesenteric lymph nodes	0.67	6.91	10

*From Wade H. Brown, Louise Pearce, and Chester M. Van Allen, *J. Exp. Med.* 43, 734–738 (1926).

Direct evidence of wide variance in human anatomy was first brought out by Barry Anson, professor of anatomy at Northwestern University, in his *Atlas of Human Anatomy*.[4] I will show only one picture from this source: one of a series of normal stomachs. This typifies the anatomical differences that exist. Great as these differences are, similar differences, often less easily depicted, exist in our endocrine glands, in our brains, and in our sense organs.

The individuality of each of us is based on solid scientific facts which cannot be controverted. Too many students of alcoholism prefer to ignore these facts and devote their attention to grandiose discussions about "man."

Postscript: At last, however, in 1980, Joseph E. Seagram & Sons, Inc., have announced a grant of $5.8 million to Harvard University Medical School to answer, essentially, the question why some individuals are "more susceptible to alcohol and alcoholism than others." This is a central problem but in my opinion has been badly neglected as the accompanying critique emphasizes.

The magnitude of this Seagram grant is a measure of the importance and complexity of the problem and it is gratifying to know that the study will be under the supervision of Dr. Bert L. Vallee, a competent investigator and a member of the National Academy of Sciences. When the role of biochemical individuality in alcoholism has been more fully explored, prevention of alcoholism will be greatly facilitated.

The second deficiency among medical scientists and others who consider the problem of alcoholism is a lack of appreciation of the intricacies of the nutritional process. In 1971 I called attention to the fact that many prominent physicians confess a high degree of ignorance in the field of nutrition and deplore this lack in their training.[5]

This deficiency becomes far more acute because of new insights into nutrition which are just now beginning to be appreciated.

After exploring with and consulting dozens of top

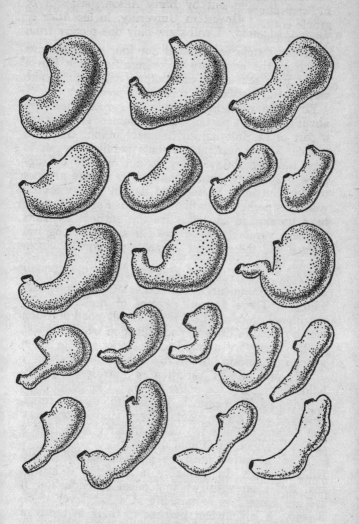

VARIATIONS IN "NORMAL" HUMAN STOMACHS

From *Atlas of Human Anatomy* by Barry J. Anson, W. B. Saunders Co., Philadelphia, 1951.

authorities in the field, my colleagues and I published in *Perspectives in Biology and Medicine* a fifteen-page article entitled "A Renaissance of Nutritional Science Is Imminent."[6]

In this article we pointed out four novel insights which in the aggregate make nutrition look like a brand new science. I can outline only briefly here without full justification these four points.

First, the nutrient elements, of which there are about forty, are a part of our environment and become a part of the internal environment of our cells and tissues. These nutrient elements parallel oxygen in their indispensability. They do not need to be supplied by the environment minute by minute as does oxygen, but must be supplied day by day, week by week, or perhaps month by month. For oxygen we have no storage capacity; for the nutrient elements we have varying storage capacities. In the long run oxygen and the nutrient elements are equally essential to life.

Second, for reasons which become obvious, the cellular environments in our bodies are never *perfectly* adjusted. There are all degrees of quality in the nutritional process. There is not simply good nutrition which promotes life and poor nutrition which induces death. There are a hundred gradations in between which may sustain life but to a suboptimal degree.

This principle of variation of nutritional quality holds throughout the entire biological kingdom. It is experienced by mammals, fowls, fish, insects, fungi, bacteria, and green plants. Every kind of organism can be and often is fed and kept alive at at least a dozen levels of nutritional quality.

Third, attention must be paid to *individual* nutritional needs. Individuality in nutrition is just as real and meaningful as anatomical individuality. If we are content to sustain life at a low level of efficiency, it is sufficient perhaps to think in terms of *man's* nutritional needs. If our aim is higher than merely to keep people alive, individual needs must be considered.

Further, nutrients should not be thought of as

"magic bullets" or medicines that cure diseases. All the nutrient elements (all forty of them), along with oxygen and water, act as a *team* to promote life and health. Every one of the nutrient elements is an essential *part* of the machinery of living matter. The different nutrients are analogous to the nuts, bolts, spindles, and gears in a complex machine.

Inferior nutrition results when the *team* is weak because of relative deficiencies and imbalances. Life cannot continue if any essential cog is absolutely missing. The metabolic machinery can limp along when there are relative lacks.

These newer insights into the nutritional process must be considered in connection with the relationship between nutrition and alcoholism. These insights place the whole situation in an entirely different light. Certainly questions which desperately need to be fully explained are these: While it is universally recognized that alcoholics are commonly deficient in a number of nutrients, is it clear that this poorly nourished condition has nothing to do with the maintenance of their alcoholic condition? Does the progressive deterioration of a pre-alcoholic's nutritional status have nothing to do with his becoming an alcoholic?

The newer nutritional insights as set forth in more detail in my newly published *Physicians' Handbook of Nutritional Science*[7] make the nutritional approach to alcoholism a "new ball game."

It is obvious, in the light of these insights, that we have no basis for expecting that niacinamide, thiamin, pantothenic acid, tryptophan, zinc, or any other nutrient will serve as a remedy for the alcoholic condition or will bring about its general prevention. But *what about the complete nutritional team?* This has never been tried with any reasonable degree of expertness.

A reasonable hypothesis is this: Really excellent nutrition will prevent alcoholism from developing and will promote maximum rehabilitation to those who are already afflicted.

Another way of stating essentially the same hypothesis is this: Expert control of the total environment of the cells and tissues of our bodies and brains will prevent the development of the diseased condition we call alcoholism and will help repair its damage.

In still other words: We hypothesize that the cells in our bodies and in our brains are genetically capable of remaining well. All they need to accomplish this is a suitable environment. If this environment is of low quality, however, the stage is set for the development of alcoholism as well as other diseases.

This idea is set forth as an *hypothesis*. It is not an easy hypothesis to test. It requires expertness.

About twenty years ago in Dr. Frederick Stare's laboratory at Harvard a related hypothesis was tested, partly as a result of my cooperation.[8] Certain vitamins were tested for their effectiveness in promoting sobriety in alcoholics.

The results showed some definite promise but they left much to be desired. From the standpoint of the newer insights into nutrition, the experiment was seriously faulty because the "magic bullet" concept was being explored. The vital teamwork principle is yet to be applied to the prevention and cure of alcoholism.

Recently in our laboratory we have tested the efficacy of the teamwork principle in connection with a totally different disease.[9] Rats fed certain diets regularly developed cataracts in their eyes. No single nutrient or simple combination of them will prevent these cataracts from forming. Yet using the same cataract-inducing diet we were able to prevent cataract formation one hundred percent by supplementation in such a way as to insure the presence in the diet of the *complete nutritional team*.

Recently a near-miraculous case of the application of the teamwork principle has come to my attention. Dr. Ruth Harrell of Norfolk, Virginia, a most progressive psychologist of long-standing reputation, has written me about Gary, a seven-year-old idiot boy. He still wore diapers, could not recognize people, nor could he utter a word. By exacting enzymatic analysis of his blood and biopsy specimens, Dr. Mary B. Allen, a biochemist of Richmond, Virginia, was able to spot several deficiencies in Gary's distinctive makeup. Without these the metabolic processes in his brain could not function properly. When these nutrients were supplied generously by supplementation of his diet, thus completing his nutritional team, Gary was turned on "like an electric light." He recognized people, showed an interest in things around him, and soon began to talk. Two years later he was in school and had an I.Q. of about 90.

Who knows what the results would be if serious expert attempts were made to provide alcoholics with the complete nutritional team? Nobody knows because it has never been tried. Isn't it about time for medical scientists to begin trying?

Next I come to a discussion closely related to the two topics already considered—individuality and nutrition. To me it is amazing and appalling how little attention has been paid to the *prevention* of alcoholism. On our symposium program the word *rehabilitation* occurs four times, the word *prevention* does not appear at all. This is characteristic not only of this symposium but of the vast amount of literature dealing with alcoholism, whether it be psychiatric, sociological, or biochemical in emphasis. The problem of prevention is rarely mentioned and even more rarely seriously discussed.

Probably Alcoholics Anonymous have had a major influence in this regard. They tend to draw a dividing line and attempt to help only those who affirm "I am an alcoholic." In my view it is unfortunate indeed when the general public rejects the idea of prevention and says to a potential victim in effect, "Let's wait until you are really a bona fide alcoholic." This is equivalent to saying to householders, "Let's wait until your home is fully ablaze before calling the fire department."

There are, according to estimates, ten million alcoholics in this country. There was a time when each one of these was a nonalcoholic. I have represented this transformation of a nonalcoholic to an alcoholic in a simple diagrammatic way in the accompanying illustration. Let us consider the problem briefly.

NON-ALCOHOLIC		ALCOHOLIC
Have Willpower	$\Rightarrow$	Lost Willpower
Can take it or		Can take it;
leave it		cannot leave it

Is there anything in common among the individuals who have crossed the line to become alcoholics? Is there a common denominator which applies to 100,000 to 400,000 new recruits to the alcoholic ranks each year? The answer is yes. In every single one the transformation has been accompanied by *heavy drinking*. Alcoholics do not become so overnight. For some the change may be relatively rapid (this may happen with youngsters), but usually it requires several years of heavy drinking to produce an alcoholic.

The most potent way to prevent alcoholism would be to prevent heavy drinking on the part of those who are still able to take it or leave it. If the general public were educated to know that *for very good reasons* heavy drinkers are always in danger of becoming alcoholics and that one can always protect himself by exercising moderation while he can still do so, this would bring a marked decreased in alcoholic addiction.

The reason why heavy drinking is an essential precursor of alcoholism seems to me evident. As one drinks heavily—one drink after another—his or her nutritional status gradually deteriorates. Perhaps at the start of heavy drinking an individual's nutritional process proceeds at seventy-five-percent efficiency. If this efficiency drops ten percent a year as a result of heavy drinking, in a few years the nutrition has reached a low level. He or she still remains alive, but the body and brain mechanisms are badly shot and continue to deteriorate the longer the heavy drinking continues.

Good nutrition and heavy drinking are completely antagonistic to each other. It is virtually impossible for a person to be well nourished while he or she drinks heavily. The general public is often nourished at a mediocre level of efficiency and heavy drinkers are several steps down the ladder. The prevention of alcoholism in an individual can be insured if one keeps his or her nutrition at a reasonably good level.

The newer insights into nutrition referred to earlier enter into this discussion in an important way. An article dealing with alcoholism which I consulted recently stated that a particular patient "was well nourished" merely on the basis of the fact that he had recently consumed food. In other words he was not starving.

Such illiteracy about the nutritional process as this will have to be abolished before we can make progress in determining the real meaning of "good nutrition." Even nutrition surveys, for example, give us only meagre information about the quality of the nutrition of the population surveyed. If there are no flagrant deficiencies (among the better known nutrients) the population may be judged to be well nourished, while as a matter of fact the large majority of the population may be nourished at a mediocre level, and some of the members of the population may be very poorly nourished indeed.

Our standards of nutritional excellence need to be clarified and raised on the basis of *expert* knowledge. This idea finds a parallel in the field of plant nutrition. When a field of growing corn produces thirty-five to forty bushels per acre an uninitiated opinion might be that the corn was receiving good nutrition. An expert, however, knows that if the same corn received really good nutrition it would produce at least two hundred bushels per acre.

We are faced with a problem of widespread nutritional illiteracy. When this is abolished our chances of preventing alcoholism will be vastly increased.

In summary, I wish to point out that the three deficient aspects of alcoholism research to which I have called attention—individuality, nutrition, and prevention—are worthy of careful attention in connection with many problems other than alcoholism. Every competent pharmacologist knows that drug actions are often highly individual. The study of drug addiction and of the action of psychodynamic drugs has to be of limited value until the biochemical individuality of the subjects is recognized and studied.

Expert attention to nutrition may be very effective in connection with many diseases other than alcoholism. When the internal environment of the cells and tissues of our body and brain is of mediocre quality, we remain alive, but at the same time may suffer from all sorts of unnecessary disorders.

The major triumphs of medicine have been in the area of prevention. Currently trained physicians know virtually nothing about curing smallpox, yellow fever, and the plague. They don't have to because these diseases can be prevented. The break-down, patch-up philosophy unfortunately applies at present to heart disease, dental disease, arthritis, mental retardation, alcoholism, mental illness, and "degenerative diseases" in general. As medicine advances we will learn how to *prevent* these diseases.

FOOTNOTES

1. Williams, R. J. "The Etiology of Alcoholism: A Working Hypothesis Involving the Interplay of Hereditary and Environmental Factors." *Q. J. Stud. Alcohol* 7 (1947), pp. 567–589.
2. Williams, R. J. *Biochemical Individuality*. New York: John Wiley & Sons, 1956; Austin: Univ. of Tex. Press (paperback edition), 1973.

3. Brown, W., L. Pearce, and C. Van Allen. "Organ Weights of Normal Rabbits." *J. Exp. Med. 43* (1926), pp. 738–741.

4. Anson, B. *Atlas of Human Anatomy.* Philadelphia: W. B. Saunders Co., 1951.

5. Williams, R. J. "How Can the Climate of Medical Education Be Changed?" *Persp. Biol. Med. 14* (1971), pp. 608–614.

6. Williams, R. J. "A Renaissance of Nutritional Science Is Imminent." *Persp. Biol. Med. 17* (1973), pp. 1–15.

7. Williams, R. J. *Physicians' Handbook of Nutritional Science.* Springfield, Ill.: Charles C. Thomas, 1975.

8. Trulson, M. F., R. Fleming, and F. J. Stare. "Vitamin Medication in Alcoholism." *J. Am. Med. Assoc. 155,* (1954), pp. 114–119.

9. Heffley, J. D., and R. J. Williams. "The Nutritional Teamwork Approach: Prevention and Regression of Cataracts in Rats." *Proc. Nat. Acad. Sci. USA 71* (1974), pp. 4164–4168.

BIOCHEMICAL RESEARCH ON ALCOHOLISM
(Primarily Covering the Last Decade)

Books

1. Wallgren, Henrik, and Herbert Barry. *Actions of Alcohol.* Amsterdam, New York: Elsevier Pub. Co., 1970.

2. Israel, Yedy, and Jorge Mardones, eds. *Biological Basis of Alcoholism.* New York: Wiley-Interscience, 1971.

3. Kissin, Benjamin, and Henri Begleiter, eds. *The Biology of Alcoholism.* New York: Plenum Press, 1971. Vol. I (Biochemistry).

4. Martini, G. A., and Charles Bode, eds. *Metabolic Changes Induced by Alcohol.* Berlin, New York: Springer-Verlag, 1971.

5. Roach, Mary K., Wm. M. McIsaac, and Patrick J. Creaven, eds. *Biological Aspects of Alcohol.* Austin, Texas: Univ. Tex. Press, 1971.

6. Bourne, Peter G., and Ruth Fox, eds. *Alcoholism: Progress in Research and Treatment.* New York: Academic Press, 1973.

Reviews, symposia, excerpts from books

1. "Biochemical and Nutritional Aspects of Alcoholism" (1964). Symposium sponsored by The Christopher D. Smithers Foundation and The Clayton Foundation Biochemical Institute, The University of Texas; held in New York, October 2, 1964.
2. Israel, Y., E. Rosenmann, B. Hein, G. Colombo, and M. Canessa-Fischer. "Effects of Alcohol on the Nerve Cell," in *Biological Basis of Alcoholism*, Y. Israel and J. Mardones, eds. New York: John Wiley and Sons, 1971, pp. 53–72.
3. Leevy, C. M., E. Valdellon, and F. Smith. "Nutritional Factors in Alcoholism and Its Complications," in *Biological Basis of Alcoholism*, Y. Israel and J. Mardones, eds. New York: John Wiley and Sons, 1971, pp. 365–382.
4. Mendelson, J. "Biochemical Mechanisms of Alcohol Addiction," *The Biology of Alcoholism*, B. Kissin and H. Begleiter, eds. New York: Plenum Press, 1971, Vol. I, pp. 513–544.
5. Feldstein, A. "The Effect of Alcohol on Neurohumoral Amine Metabolism." Ibid., pp. 127–161.
6. French, S. W. "Acute and Chronic Toxicity of Alcohol." Ibid., pp. 437–512.
7. Truitt, E. B., and M. J. Walsh. "The Role of Acetaldehyde in the Actions of Alcohol." Ibid., pp. 162–196.
8. Vitale, J. J., and J. Coffey. "Alcohol and Vitamin Metabolism." Ibid., pp. 327–352.
9. von Wartburg, J. P. "The Metabolism of Alcohol in Normals and Alcoholics: Enzymes." Ibid., pp. 63–102.
10. Hawkins, R. C., and H. Kalant. "The Metabolism of Ethanol and Its Metabolic Effects." *Pharmacol. Rev.* 24 (1972), pp. 67–157.
11. Seixas, Frank A., et al., eds. *Nature and Nurture in Alcoholism*, National Council on Alcoholism Conference, April 27–28, 1971. *N.Y. Acad. Sci. 197* (1972), pp. 1–229.
12. Wallgren, H. "Neurochemical Aspects of Tolerance to and Dependence on Ethanol," in *Alcohol Intoxication and Withdrawal: Experimental Studies*, Milton M. Gross, ed. New York: Plenum Press, 1973, pp. 15–31.
13. Davis, V. E., J. L. Cashaw, and K. D. McMurtrey.

"Disposition of Catecholamine-Derived Alkaloids in Mammalian Systems." Second Biannual International Symposium on Experimental Studies of Alcohol Intoxication and Withdrawal. *Proceedings 20th International Symposium on the Prevention and Treatment of Alcoholism 20* (1974), pp. 10–20.

14. Lahti, R. A. "Alcohol, Aldehydes and Biogenic Amines," in *Biochemical Pharmacology of Ethanol*, E. Majchrowicz, ed. New York: Plenum Press, 1975, pp. 239–253.

15. Roach, M. K. "Microsomal Ethanol Oxidation: Activity in Vitro and in Vivo." Ibid., pp. 33–56.

16. Thurman, R. G., and W. R. McKenna. "Pathways of Ethanol Metabolism in Perfused Rat Liver." Ibid., pp. 57–76.

JOURNAL ARTICLES

(a) *Alcohol metabolism*

1. Lieber, C. S., and L. M. DeCarli. "The Significance and Characterization of Hepatic Microsomal Ethanol Oxidation in the Liver." *Drug Metabolism and Disposition 1* (1973), pp. 428–440.

2. Korsten, M. A., S. Matouzaki, L. Feinman, and C. S. Lieber. "High Blood Acetaldehyde Levels After Ethanol Administration: Differences Between Alcoholic and Nonalcoholic Subjects." *New Engl. J. Med. 292* (1975), pp. 386–389.

3. Raskin, N. H. "Alcoholism or Acetaldehydism?" (Editorial) Ibid., pp. 442–423.

(See extensive coverage of this topic in the books and reviews cited above. In *The Biology of Alcoholism*, for example, there are about 250 citations on this subject appended to Chapter II alone.)

(b) *Liver and alcohol*

1. Lieber, C. S., and L. M. DeCarli. "Hepatic Microsomal Ethanol Oxidizing System." *J. Biol. Chem. 245* (1970), pp. 2505–2512.

2. Lieber, C. S. "Alcohol, Nutrition and the Liver." *Am. J. Clin. Nutr. 26* (1973), pp. 1163–1165.

3. Lieber, C. S. "Liver Adaptation and Injury in Alcoholism." *New Engl. J. Med.* 288 (1973), pp. 356–362.
4. Bernstein, J., L. Videla, and Y. Israel. "Role of the Sodium Pump in the Regulation of Liver Metabolism in Experimental Alcoholism." *Ann. N. Y. Acad. Sci.* 248 (1974), pp. 560–572.
5. Lieber, C. S. "Effect of Ethanol on Lipid Metabolism." *Lipids* 9 (1974), pp. 103–116.
6. Bernstein, J., L. Videla, and Y. Israel. "Hormonal Influences in the Development of the Hypermetabolic State of the Liver Produced by Chronic Administration of Ethanol." *J. Pharmacol. Exp. Therap.* 192 (1975), pp. 583–591.
7. Lieber, C. S., L. M. DeCarli, and E. Rubin. "Sequential Production of Fatty Liver, Hepatitis and Cirrhosis in Sub-Human Primates Fed Ethanol with Adequate Diets." *Proc. Nat. Acad. Sci. USA* 72 (1975), pp. 437–441.

(c) *Central Nervous System and Alcohol*

(Extensive coverage of this topic is to be found in the books and reviews cited above.)

(d) *Genetic aspects*

1. Thiessen, D. D., and D. A. Rodgers. "Alcohol Injection, Grouping, and Voluntary Alcohol Consumption of Inbred Strains of Mice." *Q. J. Stud. Alcohol* 26 (1965), pp. 278–383.
2. Winokur, G., T. Reich, J. Rimmer, and F. N. Pitts. "Alcoholism, III: Diagnosis and Familiar Psychiatric Illness in 259 Alcoholic Probands." *Arch. Gen. Psychiatry* 23 (1970), pp. 104–111.
3. Goodwin, D. W. "Is Alcoholism Hereditary?" *Arch. Gen. Psychiatry* 25 (1971), pp. 595–598.
4. Schuckit, M. A., D. W. Goodwin, and G. Winokur. "A Study of Alcoholism in Half Siblings." *Am. J. Psychiatry* 128 (1972), pp. 122–126.
5. Goodwin, D. W., F. Schulsinger, H. Moller, L. Hermansen, G. Winokur, and S. B. Guze. "Drinking Problems in Adopted and Nonadopted Sons of Alcoholics." *Arch. Gen. Psychiatry* 31 (1974), pp. 164–169.

6. Goodwin, D. W., F. Schulsinger, L. Hermansen, S. B. Guze, and G. Winokur. "Alcohol Problems in Adoptees Raised Apart from Alcoholic Biological Parents." *Arch. Gen. Psychiatry 32* (1975), pp. 238–243.

7. Randall, C. L., and D. Lester. "Alcohol Selection by DBA and C57BL Mice Arising from Ova Transfers." *Nature 255* (1975), pp. 147–148.

8. Randall, C. L., and D. Lester. "Social Modification of Alcohol Consumption in Inbred Mice." *Science 189* (1975), pp. 149–151.

(e) *Miscellaneous*

1. Siegel, F. L., M. K. Roach, and L. R. Pomeroy. "Plasma Amino Acid Patterns in Alcoholism: The Effects of Ethanol Loading." *Proc. Nat. Acad. Sci. USA 51* (1964), pp. 605–611.

2. Roach, Mary K., and R. J. Williams. "Impaired and Inadequate Glucose Metabolism in the Brain as an Underlying Cause of Alcoholism—An Hypothesis." *Proc. Nat. Acad. Sci. USA 56* (1966), pp. 566–571.

3. Williams, R. J. "A Broader Approach to the Prevention of Alcoholism." Presented at the 12th International Institute on the Prevention and Treatment of Alcoholism, Prague, Czechoslovakia, June 15, 1966. (Unpublished but circulated widely in mimeographed form in English, French, and Czech. Available from the author's office.)

4. Cohen, G., and M. Collins. "Alkaloids from Catecholamines in Adrenal Tissue: Possible Role in Alcoholism." *Science 167* (1970), pp. 1749–1751.

5. Alvarado-Andrade, R., E. Munoz, W. Solodkowska, J. Mardones. "Effects of Orotic Acid on Alcohol Consumption and In vivo Alcohol Metabolism in Rats." *Q. J. Stud. Alcohol 33* (1972), pp. 14–21.

6. Goldstein, D. B. "An Animal Model for Testing Effects of Drugs on Alcohol Withdrawal Reactions." *J. Pharmacol. Exp. Therap. 183* (1972), pp. 14–22.

7. Kaplan, R., S. Blume, S. Rosenberg, J. Pitrelli, and W. J. Turner. "Phenytoin, Metronidazole and Multivitamins in the Treatment of Alcoholism." *Q. J. Stud. Alcohol 33* (1972), pp. 97–104.

8. Olivecrona, T., O. Hernell, O. Johnson, G. Fex, L. Wallinder, and O. Sandgren. "Effect of Ethanol on

Some Enzymes Inducible by Fat-Free Refeeding." *Q. J. Stud. Alcohol 33* (1972), pp. 1–13.

9. Halstead, C. H., E. A. Robles, and E. Mezey. "Intestinal Malabsorption in Folate Deficient Alcoholics." *Gastroenterology 64* (1973), pp. 526–532.

10. Wynder, E. L., and K. Mabuchi. "Etiological and Environmental Factors of Cancer of the Gastrointestinal Tract, Esophagus." *J. Am. Med. Assoc. 226* (1973), pp. 1546–1548.

11. Dohrzanski, T. "Endocrine Alterations in Delirium Tremens." *Q. J. Stud. Alcohol 35* (1974), pp. 1205–1211.

12. Feigenbaum, P. A., and C. E. Becker. "Feminization in Male Alcoholics." *New Engl. J. Med. 291* (1974), p. 915.

13. Kekki, M., P. Pentikainen, and O. Mustola. "Effect of Acute and Prolonged Ethanol Administration on Serotonin Metabolism and Excretion in Urine and Bile of Rats." *Q. J. Stud. Alcohol 35* (1974), pp. 1195–1204.

14. Knee, S. T., and J. Razani. "Acute Organic Brain Syndrome: A Complication of Disulfiram Therapy." *Am. J. Psychiatry 131* (1974), p. 1281.

15. Lahti, R. A., and E. Majchrowicz. "Ethanol and Acetaldehyde Effects on Metabolism and Binding of Biogenic Amines." *Q. J. Stud. Alcohol 35* (1974), pp. 1–14.

16. Lowenfels, A. B. "Alcohol and Cancer." *N. Y. St. J. Med. 74* (1974), pp. 56–59.

17. Lumeng, L., and T. K. Li. "Vitamin B_6 Metabolism in Chronic Alcohol Abuse: Pyridoxal Phosphate Levels in Plasma and the Effects of Acetaldehyde on Pyridoxal Phosphate Synthesis and Degradation in Human Erythrocytes." *J. Clin. Invest. 53* (1974), pp. 693–704.

18. Sze, P. Y., J. Yanai, and B. E. Ginsburg. "Adrenal Glucocorticoids as a Required Factor in the Development of Ethanol Withdrawal Seizures in Mice." *Grain Res. 80* (1974), pp. 155–159.

19. Ulett, G. A., E. Itil, and S. G. Perry. "Cytotoxic Food Testing in Alcoholics." *Q. J. Stud Alcohol 35* (1974), pp. 930–942.

20. Van-Thiel, D. H., J. Bavales, and R. Lester. "Ethanol Inhibition of Vitamin A Metabolism in the Testes: Pos-

sible Mechanism for Sterility in Alcoholics." *Science 186* (1974), pp. 941–942.

21. Hillborn, M., and Kurte, M. "Does Ethanol Intoxication Promote Brain Infarction in Young Adults?" *Lancet 2* (1978), pp. 1181–1183.

22. von Wartburg, J. P. "Biochemical Aspects of Alcoholism." *Chimia 33* (1979).

Appendix III

Bibliographies
for This Book

GENERAL BIBLIOGRAPHY ON ALCOHOLISM

A complete bibliography on the subject would be extensive indeed. Some conception of its scope will be gained by perusing the bibliographic material in Appendix I.

Titles related to the support of the general thesis of this book.

1. Jetter, W. W. "Diagnosis of Acute Alcohol Intoxication by a Correlation of Clinical and Chemical Findings." *Am. J. Med. Sci. 196* (1938), p. 475.
2. Williams, Roger J. "The Etiology of Alcoholism: A Working Hypothesis Involving the Interplay of Hereditary and Environmental Factors." *Q. J. Stud. Alcohol 7* (1947), pp. 567-587. (See Appendix I.)
3. Williams, R. J. "Alcoholics and Metabolism." *Sci. Am. 179* (1948), pp. 50–53.
4. Williams, R. J., L. J. Berry, and E. Beerstecher, Jr. "Individual Metabolic Patterns, Alcoholism, Genetotrophic Diseases." *Proc. Nat. Acad. Sci. 35* (1949), pp. 265–271.
5. Williams, R. J., E. Beerstecher, Jr., and L. J. Berry. "The Concept of Genetotrophic Disease." *Lancet 258* (1950), pp. 287–289.
6. Beerstecher, E., Jr., H. E. Sutton, H. K. Berry, W. D. Brown, J. Reed, G. B. Rich, L. J. Berry, and R. J. Williams. "Biochemical Individuality. V. Explorations

with Respect to the Metabolic Patterns of Compulsive Drinkers." *Arch. Biochem.* 29 (1950), pp. 27–40.

7. Williams, R. J. *Nutrition and Alcoholism.* Norman, Oklahoma: Univ. of Oklahoma Press, 1951. (Out of print but available in some libraries.)

8. Williams, R. J. "Alcoholism as a Nutritional Problem." *J. Clin. Nutr. 1* (1952), pp. 32–36.

9. Ravel, J. M., B. Felsing, E. M. Lansford, Jr., R. H. Trubey, and W. Shive. "Reversal of Alcohol Toxicity by Glutamine." *J. Biol. Chem. 214* (1955), p. 497.

10. Rogers, L. L., R. B. Pelton, and R. J. Williams. "Voluntary Alcohol Consumption by Rats Following Administration of Glutamine." *J. Biol. Chem. 214* (1955), pp. 503–506.

11. Williams, R. J., R. B. Pelton, and L. L. Rogers. "Dietary Deficiencies in Animals in Relation to Voluntary Alcohol and Sugar Consumption." *Q. J. Stud. Alcohol 16* (1955), pp. 234–244.

12. Williams, R. J. "The Genetotrophic Approach to Alcoholism." *Origins of Resistance to Toxic Agents,* Proc. of Symposium held in Wash., D.C., March 25–27, 1954. New York: Academic Press, 1955.

13. Williams, R. J. "Biochemical Approach to the Study of Personality." *Psychiatric Research Rep. 2* (1955), pp. 31–37.

14. Rogers, L. L., R. B. Pelton, and R. J. Williams. "Amino Acid Supplementation and Voluntary Alcohol Consumption by Rats." *J. Biol. Chem. 220* (1956), pp. 321–323.

15. Williams, R. J. "Biochemical Individuality—An Inescapable Basic Factor in the Alcoholism Problem." (Paper presented at International Congress in Istanbul, September, 1956.)

16. Williams, R. J. *Alcoholism: The Nutritional Approach.* Austin, Texas: Univ. of Tex. Press, 1959.

17. Williams, R. J. "Biochemical Individuality and Cellular Nutrition: Prime Factors in Alcoholism." *Q. J. Stud. Alcohol 20* (1959), pp. 452–463.

18. Williams, R. J., and F. L. Siegel. "The Physiological Effects of Alcohol in Relation to the Problem of Alcoholism." *Advances in Alcohol and Alcoholic Beverages Research,* Gl. Nosal, ed. Geneva: Pool Finsec, 1961. Vol. 2, pp. 102–117.

19. Williams, R. J. "Fundamental Considerations Relating Alcoholism to Biochemistry and Nutrition." Symposium on Biochemical and Nutritional Aspects of Alcoholism sponsored by The Christopher D. Smithers Foundation and The Clayton Foundation Biochemical Institute, The University of Texas. Held in New York, October 2, 1964. "Glutamine as a General Metabolic Agent Protecting Against Alcohol Poisoning," William Shive, Ph.D. (Chairman, Department of Chemistry, and Clayton Foundation Biochemical Institute, University of Texas, Austin). "Experiments in Treating Alcoholics with Glutamic Acid and Glutamine," Louis P. Fincle, M.D. (Staff Physician, Continued Treatment Service, Veterans Administration Hospital, Bedford, Mass.). "Plasma Amino Acid Patterns in Alcoholism," Frank L. Siegel, Ph.D. (Joseph P. Kennedy, Jr., Laboratory, Department of Pediatrics, University of Wisconsin Medical School, Madison). "Nutrition in the Practical Management of Alcoholics," Allen A. Parry, M.D. (Chief of Alcoholic Service, Morristown Memorial Hospital, Morristown, New Jersey). "Effects of Alcohol on Brain Metabolism," J. H. Quastel, Ph.D., D.Sc. (Department of Biochemistry, McGill University, and Director, McGill-Montreal General Hospital Research Institute, Montreal, P.Q., Canada). "Enzymatic Aspects of Alcoholism," Bert L. Vallee, M.D. (Department of Medicine, Harvard Medical School, Boston, Massachusetts). Discussant—Jack H. Mendelson, M.D. (Department of Psychiatry, Massachusetts General Hospital, Boston, Mass.). Discussant—Seymour Kety, M.D. (Chief, Laboratory of Clinical Science, National Institute of Mental Health, Bethesda, Md.).
20. Williams, R. J. *The Clayton Foundation Biochemical Institute, A Short History*. Austin, Texas: Univ. of Tex. Printing Div., 1966.
21. Roach, M. K., and R. J. Williams. "Impaired and Inadequate Glucose Metabolism in the Brain as an Underlying Cause of Alcoholism—An Hypothesis." *Proc. Nat. Acad. Sci. USA 56* (1966), pp. 566–571.
22. Williams, R. J. "A Broader Approach to the Prevention of Alcoholism." Talk presented at the 12th International Institute on the Prevention and Treatment of

Alcoholism, Prague, Czechoslovakia, 1966. (Unpublished.)

23. Williams, R. J. "The Genetotrophic Approach to Metabolic Disease," in *Exploratory Concepts in Muscular Dystrophy and Related Disorders*. Amsterdam, The Netherlands: Excerpta Med. Found. (1967), pp. 103–111.

24. Williams, R. J. "Heredity, Human Understanding and Civilization." *Am Sci*. 57 (1969), pp. 237–243.

25. Gordis, E. "What Is Alcoholism Research?" *Ann. Intern. Med.* 85 (1976), pp. 821–823.

ADDENDUM

1. *The Biology of Alcohol and Alcoholism*—A Symposium of The American Society for Experimental Pathology. Presented at the 58th Annual Meeting of the Federation of American Societies for Experimental Biology, Atlantic City, New Jersey, April 10, 1974. *Fed. Proc.* 34 (1975), pp. 2038–2075.

Chairmen: E. Rubin and E. A. Smuckler. "Alcoholic Drink, Its Production and Effect," E. A. Smuckler. "Molecular Injury to Mitochondria Produced by Ethanol and Acetaldehyde," A. I. Cedarbaum and E. Rubin. "Liver Hypermetabolic State after Chronic Ethanol Consumption: Hormonal Interrelations and Pathogenic Implications," Y. Israel, L. Videla, and J. Bernstein. "Differences in Hepatic and Metabolic Changes after Acute and Chronic Alcohol Consumption," C. S. Lieber, R. Teschke, Y. Hasumura, and L. M. DeCarli. "Significant Pathways of Hepatic Ethanol Metabolism," R. G. Thurman, W. R. McKenna, H. J. Brentzel, Jr., and S. Hesse.

2. Pittman, David J., and Archer Tongue, eds. *Handbook of Organizations for Research on Alcohol and Alcoholism Problems*. Imp. Express, Pully, 1963.

3. Lieber, Charles S., ed. *Metabolic Aspects of Alcoholism*. Baltimore: University Park Press, 1976.

4. Armor, D. J., J. M. Polich, and H. B. Stambul. *Alcoholism and Treatment*. A report resulting from the Rand Corporation study on alcoholism and treatment. This report was sponsored by a grant from the Na-

tional Institute of Alcohol Abuse and Alcoholism, HEW, Santa Monica, CA: Rand Corporation, 1976.

5. *Finnish Foundation for Alcohol Studies: Report on Activities 1973–1977* (1977). This report contains a list of 27 publications of the Foundation itself, as well as a bibliography of some 570 publications covering Finnish alcohol research during the period 1972–1976–77. Although a significant number of these papers are available in English, the majority are published in Finnish.

6. Tornabene, G., and T. A. Longworthy. "Ethanol Ingestion: Differences in Blood Acetaldehyde Concentrations in Relatives of Alcoholics and Controls." *Science 203* (1978), pp. 54–55.

7. Majchrowicz, Edward, and Ernest P. Noble, eds. *Biochemistry and Pharmacology of Ethanol.* New York: Plenum Press, 1979.

Titles related to inborn individuality.

1. Loeb, Leo. *The Biological Basis of Individuality.* Springfield, Ill.: Charles C. Thomas, 1945. (The title of this book is misleading, since it deals largely with studies involving the restrictive area of transplantation of tissues. This concerns *a* biological basis of individuality.)

2. Williams, R. J. "Biochemical Individuality and Its Implications." *Chem. Eng. News 25* (1947), pp. 1112–1113.

3. Williams, R. J., et al. *Biochemical Institute Studies IV—Individual Metabolic Patterns and Human Disease: An Exploratory Study Utilizing Predominantly Paper Chromatographic Methods.* Austin, Texas: Univ. Tex. Publ. 5109, 1951.

"Introduction, General Discussion and Tentative Conclusions," Roger J. Williams. "Development of Paper Chromatography for Use in the Study of Metabolic Patterns," Helen Kirby Berry, Harry Eldon Sutton, Louise Cain, and Jim S. Berry. "The Influence of Solvent Composition, Temperature and Some Other Factors on the Rf Values of Amino Acids in Paper Chromatography," B. Jirgensons. "Quantitative Study of Urinary and Salivary Amino Acids Using Paper

Chromatography," Helen Kirby Berry and Louise Cain. "The Quantitative Determination of Histidine Using Paper Chromatography," Louise Cain and Helen Kirby Berry. "The Quantitative Determination of Creatinine in Urine Using Paper Chromatography," Helen Kirby Berry and Louise Cain. "The Quantitative Determination of Creatine in Urine by Paper Chromatography," Louise Cain. "The Quantitative Estimation of Uric Acid by Paper Chromatographic Methods, With Applications to Human Urine and Saliva," Helen Kirby Berry. "The Quantitative Estimation of Urea by Paper Chromatographic Methods With Applications to Human Urine," Helen Kirby Berry. "A Micro Determination of Sodium Using Paper Chromatography," Harry Eldon Sutton. "Quantitative Study of Ketosteroids by Paper Chromatographic Methods with Applications to Human Urine," Eric Bloch, Ernest Beerstecher, Jr., and Roy C. Thompson. "The Determination of Ferric Chloride Chromogens in Human Urine by Paper Chromatographic Methods," Harry Eldon Sutton and Ernest Beerstecher, Jr. "The Effects of Single Vitamin Deficiencies on the Consumption of Alcohol by White Rats," Ernest Beerstecher, Jr., Janet G. Reed, William Duane Brown, and L. Joe Berry. "Individual Excretion Patterns in Laboratory Rats," Janet G. Reed. "A Study of the Alcoholic Consumption and Amino Acid Excretion Patterns of Rats of Different Inbred Strains," Janet G. Reed. "A Study of the Urinary Excretion Patterns of Six Human Individuals," Helen Kirby Berry, Louise Cain, and Lorene Lane Rogers. "Further Studies on Individual Urinary and Salivary Amino Acid Patterns," Helen Kirby Berry. "Individual Urinary Excretion Patterns of Young Children," Helen Kirby Berry and Louise Cain. "A Further Study of Urinary Excretion Patterns in Relation to Diet," Harry Eldon Sutton. "Metabolic Patterns of Underweight and Overweight Individuals," Jack D. Brown and Ernest Beerstecher, Jr. "Metabolic Patterns of Schizophrenic and Control Groups," M. Kendall Young, Jr., Helen Kirby Berry, Ernest Beerstecher, Jr., and Jim S. Berry. "Exploration of Metabolic Patterns in Mentally Deficient Children," Louise Cain.

4. Williams, R. J., W. D. Brown, and R. W. Shideler. "Metabolic Peculiarities in Normal Young Men as Revealed by Repeated Blood Analysis." *Proc. Nat. Acad. Sci. USA 41* (1955), pp. 615–620.

5. Williams, R. J. *Biochemical Individuality.* New York: John Wiley, 1956. Austin, Texas: Univ. of Tex. Press, 1973.

6. Williams, R. J. "Standard Human Beings versus Standard Values." *Science 126* (1957), pp. 453–454.

7. Williams, R. J. "Normal Young Men." *Persp. Biol. Med. 1* (1957), pp. 97–104.

8. Williams, R. J. "Clinical Implications of Biochemical Differences Between Individuals." *Mod. Med. 26* (1958), pp. 134–159.

9. Williams, R. J., R. B. Pelton, H. M. Hakkinen, and L. L. Rogers. "Identification of Blood Characteristics Common to Alcoholic Males." *Proc. Nat. Acad. Sci. USA 44* (1958), pp. 216–222.

10. Williams, R. J. "Chemical Anthropology—An Open Door." *Am. Sci. 46* (1958), pp. 1–23.

11. Williams, R. J. "Individuality and Its Significance in Human Life," in *Essays on Individuality,* Felix Morley, ed. Philadelphia: Univ. of Penn. Press, 1958, pp. 125–145.

12. Pelton, R. B., R. J. Williams, and L. L. Rogers. "Metabolic Characteristics of Alcoholics. I. Response to Glucose Stress." *Q. J. Stud. Alcohol 20* (1959), pp. 28–32.

13. Siegel, F. L., and R. J. Williams. "The Use of Baby Chicks in Studying Inherent Individuality and Its Relationship to Alcoholism." *First International Conference on the Alcoholic Beverages Research, June 2–4, 1958.* C. Radouco-Thomas, ed. Lausanne: Pool Finsec S. A., 1959, pp. 35–37.

14. Williams, R. J. "Individuality of Amino Acid Needs," in *Protein and Amino Acid Nutrition,* Anthony A. Albanese, ed. New York and London: Academic Press, 1959, pp. 45–56.

15. Williams, R. J. "Etiological Research in the Light of the Facts of Individuality." *Tex. Rep. Biol. Med. 18* (1960), pp. 168–185.

16. Siegel, F. L., and R. J. Williams "Response Patterns

to Alcohol in Baby Chicks." (abstract) *Fed. Proc. 1* (1960), p. 40.

17. Williams, R. J. "Investigation of Disease Resistance and the Mathematical Problem of Patterns." *Proc. Nat. Acad. Sci. USA 47* (1961), pp. 221–224.

18. Williams, R. J., and F. L. Siegel. " 'Propetology,' a New Branch of Medical Science." *Am. J. Med. 31* (1961), pp. 325–327.

19. Williams, R. J. "Biochemical and Physiological Variations Within Groups of Supposedly Homogeneous Experimental Animals." Symposium on Factors Involved in Host-Agent Relationships, Ames, Iowa, 1961.

20. Williams, R. J., R. B. Pelton, and F. L. Siegel. "Individuality as Exhibited by Inbred Animals; Its Implications for Human Behavior." *Proc. Nat. Acad. Sci. USA 48* (1962), pp. 1461–1466.

21. Williams R. J., and R. B. Pelton. "Individuality in Nutrition: Effects of Vitamin A-Deficient and Other Deficient Diets on Experimental Animals." *Proc. Nat. Acad. Sci. USA 55* (1966), pp. 126–134.

22. Williams, R. J., and G. Deason. "Individuality in Vitamin C Needs." *Proc. Nat. Acad. Sci. USA 57* (1967), pp. 1638–1641.

23. Gutierrez, R. M., and R. J. Williams. "Excretion of Ketosteroids and Proneness to Breast Cancer." *Proc. Nat. Acad. Sci. USA 59* (1968), pp. 938–943.

24. Storr, E. E., and R. J. Williams. "A Study of Monozygous Quadruplet Armadillos in Relation to Mammalian Inheritance." *Proc. Nat. Acad. Sci. USA 60* (1968), pp. 910–914.

25. Williams, R. J. "Biochemical Individuality: A Story of Neglect." *J. Internat. Acad. Prev. Med. 1:2* (1974), pp. 99–106.

26. Williams, R. J. "The Biology of Behavior." *Saturday Reviw,* Jan. 30 (1971), p. 17. (18 permissions to reprint.)

27. Williams, R. J. "A Case for Intuition and Common Sense," in *Legacies in the Study of Behavior,* Josephy Warren Cullen, ed. Springfield, Ill.: Charles C Thomas, 1974, pp. 211–246.

Doctoral dissertations related to inborn individuality.

1. Bloch, Eric. "I. The Effect of Dietary Supplementation Upon the Growth and Reproduction of Individual Mice of Three Strains Fed an Adequate Diet." Univ. of Texas at Austin, 1953.

2. Ripperton, Lyman A. "A Study of Urinary Excretion Patterns of Diabetic Individuals." Univ. of Texas at Austin, 1953.

3. Brown, William D. "Individual Patterns in Normal Humans; Organic Blood Constituents." Univ. of Texas at Austin, 1955.

4. Shideler, Robert W. "Individual Differences in Mineral Metabolism." Univ. of Texas at Austin, 1956.

5. Doebbler, Gerald F. "Biochemical Individuality: Urinary Sulfur Patterns." Univ. of Texas at Austin, 1957.

6. Hakkinen, Hertta-Maija. "A Study of Some Metabolic Patterns in Alcoholic and Schizophrenic Individuals." Univ. of Texas at Austin, 1957.

7. Siegel, Frank L. "Individuality in Baby Chicks as Related to Their Responses to Alcohol." Univ. of Texas at Austin, 1960.

8. Storrs, Eleanor E. "Individuality in Monozygotic Quadruplets of the Armadillo, *Dasypus Novemcinctus,* Linn." Univ. of Texas at Austin, 1967.

9. Pomeroy, Leon R. "Computer Assisted Electroencephalographic Analysis of Chick Pyridoxine Deficiency States." Univ. of Texas at Austin, 1967.

10. Gutierrez, Rose M. "Gas Chromatographic Determination of Urinary 17-Ketosteroids in Postoperative Breast Cancer Subjects." Univ. of Texas at Austin, 1967.

11. Dunlop, David S. "The Problem of Sleep and Wakefulness: Biochemical Aspects. Oxidative N-dealkylase Systems in Individual Rats." Univ. of Texas at Austin, 1968.

12. Heffley, James D. "Amino Acid Patterns in Hamster Serum in Relation to Age, Diet, and Ethanol Consumption." Univ. of Texas at Austin, 1970.

13. Bode, Charles W. "Effects of Nicotinamide on the Pharmacodynamic Activity of Ethanol in Inherently Sensitive and Resistant Mice." Univ. of Texas at Austin, 1976.

Titles related to the role of nutrition.

1. Williams, R. J. "Human Nutrition and Individual Variability." *Borden's Review of Nutrition Research 17* (1956), pp. 11–26.

2. Williams, R. J. "A Nutritional Approach to Alcoholism." *First International Conference on the Alcoholic Beverages Research, June 2–4, 1958.* C. Radouco-Thomas, ed. Lausanne: Pool Finsec S. A., 1959, pp. 29–34.

3. Williams, R. J. "The Expanding Horizon in Nutrition." *Tex. Rep. Biol. Med. 19* (1961), pp. 245–258.

4. Williams, R. J. *Nutrition in a Nutshell.* Garden City, New York: Doubleday, 1962.

5. Williams, R. J. "The Individual Approach to Geriatric Nutrition." (1969). (Paper presented to Council on Aging and Human Development at Duke Medical Center, Feb. 13, 1968.) Reprinted from the *Duke University Council on Aging and Human Development: Proceedings of Seminars 1965–69.*

6. Williams, R. J. "Your Extraordinary Nutrition." *National Health Federation Bulletin,* No. XV. (1969), pp. 9–14. No reprints.

7. Williams, R. J. "Nutrition and Ischemic Heart Disease." *Borden's Review of Nutrition Research 31* (1971).

8. Williams, R. J. "How Can the Climate in Medical Education Be Changed?" *Persp. Bio. Med. 14* (1971), pp. 608–614.

9. Williams, R. J. " 'Supernutrition' as a Strategy for the Control of Disease." *J. Orthomolec. Psychiatry 1* (1972), pp. 98–103.

10. Williams, R. J. *Nutrition Against Disease.* New York: Bantam, 1973.

11. Williams, R. J., J. D. Heffley, and C. W. Bode. "The Nutritive Value of Single Foods." *Proc. Nat. Acad. Sci. USA 68* (1971), pp. 2361–2364.

12. Williams, R. J. (with technical assistance of C. W. Bode). "Should the Science-based Food Industry Be Expected to Advance?" in *Orthomolecular Psychiatry,* David Hawkins and Linus Pauling, eds. San Francisco, Calif.: W. H. Freeman & Co., 1973, pp. 316–324.

13. Williams, R. J., and J. D. Heffley, M-L. Yew, and

C. W. Bode. "The 'Trophic' Value of Foods." *Proc. Nat. Acad. Sci. USA 70* (1973), pp. 710–713.

14. Williams, R. J., J. D. Heffley, M-L. Yew, and C. W. Bode. "A Renaissance of Nutritional Science Is Imminent." *Persp. Biol. Med. 17* (1973), p. 1–15.

15. Williams, R. J. "The Neglect of Nutritional Science in Cancer Research." *Congressional Record* (Wednesday, Oct. 16, 1974), p. S.19204.

16. Heffley, J. D., and R. J. Williams. "The Nutritional Teamwork Approach: Prevention and Regression of Cataracts in Rats." *Proc. Nat. Acad. Sci. USA 71* (1974), pp. 4164–4168.

17. Williams, R. J. "Medical Research Leading to the Acceptance of the Orthomolecular Approach." *J. Orthomolec. Psychiatry 4* (1975), pp. 98–101.

18. Williams, R. J. "Nutrition in the Prevention of Disease." (Text of Hogan Memorial Lecture delivered in Columbia, Mo., Feb. 1973.) *Baroda J. Nutr. 2* (1975), pp. 1–7.

19. Williams, R. J. "A New Brand of Nutritional Science," in *New Dynamics of Preventive Medicine*, Leon R. Pomeroy, ed. (Selected papers from the 8th meeting of The International Academy of Preventive Medicine.) (1976), pp. 91–100.

20. Williams, R. J. *Physicians' Handbook of Nutritional Science*. Springfield, Ill.: Charles C. Thomas, 1975.

21. Williams, R. J. "Inborn Individuality and Nutrition." *J. Intern. Acad. Prev. Med. 2:4* (1975), pp. 5–7.

22. Davis, D. R., and R. J. Williams. "Potentially Useful Criteria for Judging Nutritional Adequacy." *J. Clin. Nutr. 29* (1976), pp. 710–715.

23. Williams, R. J. *The Wonderful World Within You: Your Inner Nutritional Environment*. New York: Bantam Books, 1977.

Index

How's Your Health?

Bantam publishes a line of informative books, written by top experts to help you toward a healthier and happier life.

Bantam Book Catalog

Here's your up-to-the-minute listing of over 1,400 titles by your favorite authors.

This illustrated, large format catalog gives a description of each title. For your convenience, it is divided into categories in fiction and non-fiction—gothics, science fiction, westerns, mysteries, cookbooks, mysticism and occult, biographies, history, family living, health, psychology, art.

So don't delay—take advantage of this special opportunity to increase your reading pleasure.

Just send us your name and address and 50¢ (to help defray postage and handling costs).

BANTAM BOOKS, INC.
Dept. FC, 414 East Golf Road, Des Plaines, Ill. 60016

Mr./Mrs./Miss_____
(please print)

Address_____

City_____State_____Zip_____

Do you know someone who enjoys books? Just give us their names and addresses and we'll send them a catalog too!

_____

Mr./Mrs./Miss_____

Address_____

City_____State_____Zip_____

_____

Mr./Mrs./Miss_____

Address_____

City_____State_____Zip_____

FC—9/78